AFTER THE AI

AFTER THE AI

A Guide to Taking the Stage IV and Intermediate Teaching Examinations

JULIE BASIL BHSI

THRESHOLD BOOKS

First published privately by
the author, 1984

This edition published by
Threshold Books Ltd
661 Fulham Road
London
SW6 5PZ
1988

British Library Cataloguing in Publication Data
Basil, Julie
After the A.I.: a guide to taking the stage IV and intermediate teaching examinations.—2nd ed.
1. Great Britain. Livestock. Horses. Riding Instructors.
Professional education.
British Horse Society examinations
I. Title
798.2′3′076

ISBN 0-901366-45-5

Typeset by Rapid Communications Ltd, London WC1
Printed by Adlard & Son Ltd, Letchworth, Herts

CONTENTS

PREFACE

After the AI was originally intended as a modest notebook to give readers some broad idea of what they would need to know before attempting their Stage IV and Intermediate teaching examinations.

In revising it, I have updated it in accordance with the changes made in the exam syllabii last year. I have added a little here and there but have tried to avoid producing a very lengthy and detailed textbook. After a number of years training students for exams I find many such books tend to be left unread or are skimmed through by busy and often tired horsey people.

I hope I have covered most of the necessary areas of knowledge required. I have not included breeding, which has been well documented in many previous books (see later list of recommended reading), nor an explanation of the physiology of the horse, which is described in much detail in *Horse and Stable Management* by J. Houghton Brown and V. Powell Smith.

Julie Basil
December, 1987

Acknowledgements

I would like to take this opportunity of thanking the people who have advised and helped me with this book. Firstly, Dorothy Johnson, who, with her usual tact, kindness and good humour patiently offered much guidance and advice; Stephen Clarke, who found time in the midst of a busy competition season to read and offer many helpful suggestions on the flatwork section; The British Horse Society for their kind permission to reproduce their examination details; Pelham Books for allowing me to reproduce an extract from Lucinda Green's fascinating book, *Four Square*; and last, but by no means least, I am very grateful to my husband Victor and artist Dianne Breeze for their work on the diagrams.

1.

LUNGEING

I have chosen to start with this subject because lungeing is the horse's initial formal training, the object of which is to establish in the horse obedience to the trainer's aids, namely the voice, the whip and the lunge rein. As a famous dressage trainer remarked at a lecture demonstration: 'By lungeing the horse we establish at the very beginning of his training the pecking order.' It is very important that any serious rider who wishes to produce horses correctly, enabling them to participate in their chosen field of equestrianism efficiently and successfully, should take considerable time and trouble learning how to make the horse work on the lunge. The ability to lunge well is almost always the result of having a really experienced and skilled adviser at hand, coupled with the opportunity to practise on a fair number of different horses, including some who do not take an entirely co-operative attitude to the job.

Reasons for lungeing

1. Before backing the horse.

- **(a)** Teaches the horse obedience to the lunge whip and the voice.
- **(b)** Horse learns to work on a circle.
- **(c)** The horse learns to work in a regular rhythm.
- **(d)** The horse begins to find his balance and becomes more supple on the circle.
- **(e)** The horse learns to accept the contact of the lunge line and later to seek the contact of the side reins.
- **(f)** To develop the back muscles by correct work to enable him to carry the rider's weight without difficulty.

2. For exercise.
Useful when the horse has an accident or illness which prevents him from being ridden (e.g. girth galls) or when a suitable rider is not available.
3. Overcoming problems and improving the horse during training. The tense horse may become calmer on the lunge, finds a better rhythm and the paces may improve as a result.
4. Lungeing the rider.
(a) The beginner. Used to give confidence in the initial stages and to teach a firm basic position.
(b) The improver. Used with the more experienced rider to improve balance, straightness, suppleness and depth of position. Useful for correcting habitual positional faults.

Essentials for safe lungeing

1. Must be in an enclosed area, otherwise some riders will feel anxious. Gives the trainer more control. Helps the horse to concentrate.
2. The surface must be level and flat and the surface should be the best available for the horse's sake (e.g. shavings and sand).
3. Avoid working on small circles – this places undue strain on horse's back and hocks and makes it difficult for the rider to sit well (no smaller than 15m).

Equipment

(a) Horse 15.2hh to 16hh ideal for lungeing most riders. Must have steady reliable temperament but not be a slug. His paces should be round, regular and rhythmic, neither flat and short nor too long and extravagant. He must be a comfortable ride and have sufficient bone to carry more than lightweight riders.
(b) Saddle A good dressage saddle or, if not available, a not-too-forward cut general-purpose saddle. A forward-cut jumping saddle will encourage the rider to draw up his knee.
(c) Bridle Simple snaffle and lungeing cavesson (loop up the reins if left on).

(d) Side reins Preferably fixed leather side reins (those with elastic inserts encourage the horse to lie on the contact). Some people prefer not to use side reins when lungeing the horse, as opposed to lungeing the rider, until the horse has reached an advanced stage of training. When working on a circle, the outside side rein is taut, the inside rein less so. Most people prefer both side reins to be of equal length but some fit the inside side rein shorter. This can encourage too much neck bend, allowing the horse to escape through the outside shoulder. The horse must not have the side reins so short that he is overbent, the corner of his mouth should be about level with his hip, depending on the conformation of the individual.

(e) Lunge line Flat webbing type best: nylon ones can cut, even through gloves. Come in two sizes: 25 and 27 feet.

(f) Lunge whip Comes in different weights and balance to suit personal preference.

(g) Boots/bandages Must be well fitting to avoid chafing. Horse should be booted or bandaged all round to protect his joints. If only one set of boots is available these are usually put on the hind legs but the decision will depend on whether the horse moves close at the front or behind.

Lungeing the horse

A roller may be used instead of a saddle. Never lunge on a slope as this puts a severe strain on the horse's joints. Lungeing in any case should be done with discretion as it is taxing on the horse and from five to thirty minutes are usually sufficient in most circumstances.

The horse must first learn to go away from the trainer on to a circle. He must respect and move forward from the lunge whip (but not be frightened of it) into a steady contact with the lunge line. If the lunge line is not constantly taut then the horse is not going forwards into a good contact on a true circle.

Once the horse will stay out on the circle, taking a steady contact, then he must be encouraged to find a constant rhythm. If he goes forward into a good contact on a true circle and works in a consistent rhythm then he must inevitably begin to find a better balance and become more supple. It follows that his working paces must, as a result, improve. The horse must learn to seek forwards for the contact, and the side reins should never be fitted so short that the horse's nose is pulled towards his chest, making him flatten his back and leave his hocks trailing.

Lungeing over poles and fences

Jumping horses on the lunge can be interesting and informative, but it does impose a great strain on the horse's hocks, as he is obliged to turn fairly sharply each time after landing. This can be avoided to some extent by the trainer moving quickly in a line parallel to the horse. It needs to be done carefully and not too frequently. It is a useful exercise with a green youngster who is either lacking in confidence or, perhaps the reverse, lacks respect and technique in his jumping. The rider can see for himself the horse's attitude on the approach to the fence and his style in the air. The anxious horse can gain confidence when not burdened by a rider (his anxiety may have come from poor or rough riding) and the careless or over-impulsive horse can be taught to respect his fences without endangering the rider. If such a horse hits a fairly solid fence hard and either stings his legs or maybe falls as a result, he cannot associate it with the rider and should learn to jump more cleanly and carefully thereafter.

Always choose good ground and, to begin with, make the fence small and inviting, 'closed' on both sides and with sloping poles to carry the lunge line over the wing of the fence. The horse must be lungeing well on the flat before attempting to jump him on the lunge.

Lungeing the rider

See 'The Lunge Lesson' in the section on teaching.

2.

Breaking and Backing

'Breaking the horse in' is the traditional expression used for the lunge work done with a young horse in preparation for backing him for the first time. It is a misleading and inapt description since it implies a certain amount of force, even aggression, towards the horse. Some horses will prove more difficult in the early stages of training on the lunge, very often because they have been mishandled or insufficiently handled as foals, yearlings and two-year-olds. Others may prove difficult for reasons of temperament – e.g. the very sharp, quick-thinking horse (often a potential star), the spooky horse, the timid horse who is genuinely lacking in confidence, and so on. Whilst it is essential to be firm so as to establish obedience in the young horse, any violent or aggressive attempts to force the horse to co-operate almost always prove unsuccessful since the horse is far stronger physically than a human being. The horse must learn to obey and co-operate with the trainer because he finds it easier and more pleasant than disobedience. The trainer will succeed best when he concentrates on using his brain rather than his brawn, for in this respect he has the advantage over the horse.

I will attempt to give an outline programme of breaking and backing a horse, but the time schedule I suggest can only be a rough guide. How long the job takes varies from one horse to another. It depends upon the horse's temperament, the trainer's experience and ability, the facilities available and even, where an indoor school is not used, the weather.

There are two slightly different opinions about the amount of time which should be spent lungeing a youngster before he is backed. Some people like to give the horse a month or even longer on the lunge. This enables the trainer to make the horse very obedient, relatively supple, and relatively fit (for many this is a disadvantage). After a month to six weeks of lungeing the young horse will be stronger and therefore more capable of removing his rider if he takes objection to someone sitting on him. In fact, not many horses do object to the rider's weight as such. The problems mostly arise when the horse finds he is expected to move with this unaccustomed burden on his back. Another disadvantage of a considerable period of lungeing before backing is the risk of putting too much strain on the horse's joints, especially the hocks. This would be particularly relevant when using a less-than-perfect working surface for the horse.

Many people prefer to lunge the horse only for as long as it takes to make the horse obedient, so that he is working confidently in all three paces on a 15-20m circle, in a good rhythm and taking a consistent contact with the lunge rein. He has, of course, to be accustomed to the tack. With a skilled trainer and a co-operative and confident horse the lungeing phase of training might only take three days. At this stage, the young horse, having been made obedient to the commands of his trainer and familiar with wearing a saddle and bridle, will be mentally ready to accept a rider; nor will he be fit or fresh. Quite simply he will be a little tired at this stage and that much quieter.

Of course three days is the minimum and for many horses a week to ten days would be needed. The actual time taken is of secondary importance. What is vital is that this first stage in the horse's training is carried out quietly, calmly and methodically, with the minimum of stress to the horse, mentally or physically. A well-broken horse is not only given a really good start to his career, whatever his field, it also stands him in good stead when the inevitable problems occur somewhere later in his training. If the newly backed horse is willing, obedient and confident then the trainer has done a good job whatever the length of time taken.

The first task when breaking the horse is to lunge him in a lungeing cavesson and, if he does not object too much, brushing boots all round. If possible this first session should be at a quiet time in a quiet place with as few distractions as possible. Later on, the horse must learn to concentrate with a certain amount of activity going on around him, but on day one peace and quiet will be most helpful to horse and trainer. Some people like to have an assistant present, but unless the horse is very big and strong and is known to be rather bossy and boisterous to handle there is usually no need for two people to hold the lunge rein.

The aim of this first lungeing session is for the horse to learn to move forwards from the whip to the contact of the lunge line. He must respect the whip, but not run away from it in fear. How much or how little voice is used when lungeing is a matter of personal choice. Many people lunge without giving any verbal commands and claim that this makes the trainer more effective in keeping the horse forwards from the whip to the hand. Most, however, use the voice as an auxiliary aid to back up the whip and hand. Over-use of the voice when the trainer constantly repeats commands in a never-ending stream of chatter is at best ineffective and at worst confusing to the horse.

This first lunge should last between ten and twenty minutes at the end of which the horse should be moving forwards in a good active trot and staying out on the circle on both reins, taking up a nice steady contact.

The next stage is to lunge the horse in a roller. It is a good idea to introduce the horse to this in the stable. It should be tightened very slowly and carefully as this frightens some horses. It is best left not too tightly fastened initially but must always be secured with a breastplate to avoid the risk of the roller slipping backwards and becoming a 'bucking strap'. The horse can be left wearing the roller in the stable for half an hour before lungeing to give him time to get used to the feel of it. Some horses have quite a bucking session when first lunged in a roller. Provided the trainer keeps calm, stays his ground and at all costs keeps hold of the lunge line, this will, in most cases, be quite short-lived. If at any stage the horse manages to get away from the trainer whilst being lunged, it is advisable to have a second person to hold the lunge to ensure that the horse does not learn that he can have his own way through using his physical strength against the trainer.

Once the horse is lungeing in the roller he will be ready for the saddle to be put on the next day. The horse should be held by the trainer whilst the assistant quietly and slowly places the saddle (with a thick numnah underneath) on his back. As with a roller, a breastplate should be worn. The girth must be done up gradually and very slowly so as not to alarm the horse. Some horses are more sensitive than others about the saddle being used for the first time, but most will have a bit of a buck and a jump around initially. As with the roller it is a case of the trainer remaining in control and keeping calm and the horse will quite quickly settle. He should be lunged at first with the stirrups tied up securely, and then with them down and loose so that he gets used to the feel of them swinging on his sides.

I have not yet mentioned the use of side reins. Some people do not believe in using side reins on young horses because of the danger of their learning to go behind the bit and overbend. The main advantage of side reins to the trainer is that they give him more control of the outside of the horse and it is less easy for the horse to turn off the circle and become out of control. Many people like to use side reins almost from the start of lungeing to encourage the horse to work with a rounded topline and into the contact of the outside rein.

It is preferable to back a horse in a quiet enclosed space. An indoor school is ideal for this as unexpected disturbances at a critical moment are less likely than when working outside. Three people are needed at this stage. The trainer should stand holding the horse's head. The rider should be fairly lightweight, but, more importantly, competent, calm and brave. It is no good putting up a nervous or novice rider just because they are small and light. The third person is there to leg up the rider (and later on put his feet into the stirrups).

With some horses it may be necessary to spend one session just legging up the rider (from both sides) and letting him lie sideways across the horse. Next the horse should be led forwards with the rider still lying across the horse, no attempt having been made yet to put his right leg over the horse's back and sit upright. Should the horse become frightened when he moves forwards carrying the rider's weight for the first time, the rider is in a good position to slide off quietly and then try again. If he sits across the horse straight away and the horse humps his back in protest at the unaccustomed feel of weight on his back, the rider may find himself deposited back on the floor. When this happens the horse has gained a tremendous psychological advantage. He may then make repeated efforts to dislodge the rider. Most young horses at some stage of their early training investigate the possibilities of removing the rider from their backs. If the rider is able to sit it out the horse will quickly accept that bucking as a disobedience is unproductive.

Once the horse can be led around the training area quietly with the rider lying across the saddle, he should be halted and the rider can now attempt to put his leg across the horse and slowly sit up. Once again the trainer leads the horse in walk on a large circle. If all is well, the horse and rider can then be lunged in walk and trot on both reins. At this stage, the trainer lungeing the horse remains in control of the horse. The rider makes no attempt to use his legs or to slow or stop the horse through the rein. Quite gradually this situation is reversed, with the rider taking over the control of the horse. When the horse is walking and trotting confidently on the lunge, moving forwards from the rider's leg and coming back to the hand, it is time for the lunge line to be taken off, side reins, if used, to be removed and for horse and rider to proceed on their own.

If the horse displays no concern or resentment when he is first leant on, backed and lunged, it will be possible to achieve riding the horse loose in this one session. If, at any stage, the horse becomes anxious or disobedient it is best to proceed more slowly and take several days before riding loose.

How far you proceed with the horse's training after this depends on individual circumstances. The rider will be influenced by the horse's physique and temperament. On balance it is usually beneficial, before roughing the youngster off for a break to mature and strengthen, to have achieved most of the following. He should be walking, trotting and cantering confidently, in a fairly large area (a 20m x 40m arena is often too small at this stage), changing the rein, allowing his rider to mount and dismount without assistance, possibly working over trotting poles and popping over a very small jump from trot. If the local roads are not too busy he should have been hacked and shown traffic. At this point most youngsters will benefit physically and mentally if they are turned away for a month or two, or even longer in some cases, before being brought back into work to continue their education. As a general rule, the bigger the horse the longer he takes to mature physically and the slower you need to proceed with his training.

3.

FLATWORK

The way the horse should go

Basic essentials

1. The horse must move freely forward (i.e. without tension or resistance) taking the best length of stride which his conformation and natural movement allow.
2. The horse should work in a well-established, even rhythm set by the rider.
3. The horse must be straight (i.e. his hind feet must follow in the same line as his forefeet on straight and curved lines).

It is important to have a very clear idea of priorities when training the horse. It is very easy to become obsessed with certain problems which are impossible to correct until the horse has understood and is obedient to other more basic lessons. To quote a very obvious example of this: it is no use spending hours struggling to get your horse to have more impulsion in his paces, if his balance is still so on his forehand that the result of your efforts is simply to make him lean over more heavily on your hand.

The horse must firstly be obedient. This means that the horse must listen and respond to the rider's legs and hands (in the young and green horse the voice will also be a necessary aid). The degree of obedience from the horse to the rider will vary according to his stage of training. The recently backed four-year-old can only be expected to respond to a fairly firm aid from the leg to move, say, from walk to trot, and he has not yet learned obedience to more sophisticated requests like moving forward and sideways in response to one leg. The advanced dressage horse's obedience is of a very much higher order. He must listen to and obey many small unobtrusive signals from the rider, often given in rapid succession (for example in a sequence of flying changes). The young horse's obedience to stop, start and steer is also governed by his limited ability to concentrate for anything but short periods of training. Later, the advanced horse must have the ability to concentrate one hundred per cent on the rider's demands for the fourteen minutes of a Grand Prix dressage test.

Secondly, the horse must move in a constant, even rhythm in all its paces. Some horses seem born with good natural rhythm, but a good rider can always produce rhythmic paces even in highly strung and excitable horses. Until the horse is working in all three basic paces with a good rhythm he cannot and should not be asked to alter the length of his steps (that is, in collected, medium and extended paces).

Thirdly, the horse must be straight. This means that unless he is performing lateral work, his hind foot must follow the path of the front foot on each side. If he is travelling on a straight line he must be perfectly straight from poll to croup, and if he is on a curve or a turn of a circle he must be bent along the line of the curve. The expression 'not straight on the circle' simply means that the horse has deviated from the line of the circle either through his shoulders or his quarters. The crooked horse is compensating for stiffness. All horses have some degree of stiffness; as training progresses they will become more supple and correspondingly have less inclination to be crooked. In the early stages of training the horse will have one side on which he is more stiff (usually the right). On this stiff side he will try to make the circles smaller by falling in on his inside shoulder. He may try to bend to the outside of the circle or his quarters may swing out. On the soft or hollow side he may fall out through the outside shoulder. The circles may become larger than intended. He may tilt his head, make too much neck bend or push his quarters to the inside of the circle.

Before the horse can be asked to work with more impulsion and therefore more brilliance it is vital that he has become obedient, rhythmic and straight and therefore to some degree, supple. It is also necessary to be certain that he is working confidently with complete absence of tension. It is not uncommon for horses, particularly those whose training has been hurried, to be performing fairly difficult movements such as shoulder-in, but they are tense in their backs, the muscles are tight, and they lack softness and swing in their paces. Impulsion must not be confused with speed. Impulsion is the controlled or stored-up energy in the hindquarters of the horse. Maximum impulsion is required for extended trot. Some forward-going, forward-thinking horses tend to have too much impulsion, which manifests itself by insufficient acceptance of the rider's leg and considerable tension throughout, often displayed by evasions in the mouth.

A system of aids

The young horse learns to respond to this very simple and basically unchanging system of signals or messages. The same aids are given throughout the training, from the newly backed horse up to the Grand Prix dressage horse.

Inside leg

Used at the girth it sends the horse forwards, asks him for more energy and more activity of the hindquarters and also for a sideways bend.

Outside leg

Used very slightly behind the girth it controls the quarters. The way it is used depends on the movement being performed:

(a) Passive, as in shoulder-in.
(b) Controlling, as when riding a circle.
(c) Asking, as in half pass.

Inside hand

Asks for a bend in the neck and at the poll.

Outside hand

Controls the rhythm of the pace and also the amount of neck bend.

Under certain circumstances (as when the horse is taking a stronger contact on the inside rein and very little or none on the outside rein) these aids may be reversed. The horse is ridden on, say, a circle on the left rein, and the rider uses the right leg and left rein to keep him on the circle. This should have the effect of making the horse take a better contact down the left rein and so he will lean less on the right rein.

All aids should be given as quickly and lightly as possible, depending on the horse's stage of training.

1. Hands

The reins should be held in the hand and not just lie in the fingers. The horse is asked to decrease the pace, i.e. make a downward transition, by a light quick closing of the hands which may be repeated several times with the young or inattentive horse. The wrists must be straight and strong to act as a buffer with horses that try to lie on the hand, so preventing the rider from leaning back behind the vertical and pulling back at the horse. The outside of the wrist should be straight while the inside should be slightly rounded and concave. The shoulders and elbows help keep the contact but must not become stiff and set.

2. Legs

The top of the inside of the lower legs lie around the horse's sides covering the girth. They keep contact at all times. How much pressure is used when applying aids depends on the horse's stage of training and temperament. When the leg is passive, i.e. not requesting, but simply in contact, maintaining forward movement, the leg should stay as still as possible so as not to confuse or numb the horse.

3. Voice

Used initially, but progressively less. Can be very helpful with excitable and nervous horses.

4. Weight

Must remain equally distributed on both seat bones. Young or weak and immature horses may need the rider to sit very lightly, even slightly off the horse's back in the early stages of training.

5. Whip

Used to back up the rider's leg when horse is inattentive or disobedient.

6. Spurs

These back up the rider's leg; in later stages of training they provide a more precise aid.

Working in

The length of time the horse needs to be worked in will vary from one horse to another and is dependent upon circumstances (e.g. how fresh the horse is, the type of weather and whether the horse is working in a familiar place or not). By and large a horse should be ready to begin serious work within ten minutes. If he is not, apart from exceptional circumstances, then there is some very basic fault in the horse's training – usually a lack of basic obedience to leg and hand. Most horses work in best in trot. Some older stiff horses respond well if cantered quietly to loosen up. The exuberant, but stiff horse can be kept calm and made more supple by some initial lateral work in walk.

In any event the rider should have the same priorities in mind. The horse must move forwards from the rider's leg and from the lightest possible aid (i.e. he must be attentive). He must find and maintain a good rhythm and he must make a lateral bend through the corners and around the circles.

Once these objectives are achieved the horse will begin to work in a rounder outline. Whether he is a four-year-old working at preliminary level or an advanced dressage horse he should be rounded over the whole of his topline from poll to croup. The young horse will work on a long platform, since he is not yet trained to bring his hind legs very far forwards underneath his body, so he will be taking much of his weight on his forehand. The more advanced horse, particularly once the rider begins to make transitions and half halts and so supple him longitudinally, will work on a shorter base with his hind legs well underneath him, enabling him to be lighter and higher at the front. Like the young horse he must be rounded along the whole of his topside and both horses must have the poll as the highest point. They must both work with confidence and be free from tension.

Any mistakes or disobediences by the horse in the working-in period should be dealt with firmly and quietly (the horse who is allowed too much liberty, say, to shy, quickly learns to play on this lack of discipline on the part of the rider and the working-in period can tend to become more and more long-drawn-out).

A horse that needs to be worked in for sixty minutes or more before performing a dressage test is putting a lot of extra strain on his legs, feet and back, particularly on a day when the ground is hard and he is competing in several tests on that day.

Assessing a strange horse on the flat

1. Riding the horse

Work the horse in the three basic paces on both reins. If one pace is very bad, do not become obsessed with this problem; try to get an overall picture of the horse's strengths and weaknesses. Find out whether he is capable of any lateral work and whether you can shorten and lengthen his steps. Assess how the horse responds to your leg. Does he try to run away from it, is he a little idle and unresponsive to one or both legs, how does he respond to your hand, i.e. does he take a nice steady soft contact equally on both reins, or does he lie heavily on one or both reins? Does he fold himself into a pretty shape with his nose in and drop the contact leaving you with fresh air in your hand?

Next think about the quality of his paces. Are they springy, athletic, scopey, or simply pleasant, rounded and rhythmic, or are they disappointingly short, flat and hurried? If the paces are poor, try to decide whether this is inherent in the horse or rather because of the way the horse is going as a result of some fault in the training.

Whilst riding turns and circles decide which side the horse is stiff on, how rhythmic and well balanced he is, or the reverse. Make progressive and then direct transitions and see how the horse responds – this usually tells you a lot about any horse.

No horse is ever perfect and no horse is totally without a redeeming feature, so try not to be carried away either by over-enthusiasm for the talented horse or by being totally critical about a less capable horse.

2. Talking about the horse

Some people find it very much easier to ride a horse than to talk about what they felt and did whilst riding him. The following is a suggested plan to help make your assessment reasonably accurate and concise. It is only a suggested guideline, not a rigid set of rules.

(a) Description

Always age the horse before you ride him, otherwise you may well fall into the trap of thinking a mature but ill-educated horse is a green youngster! Give his approximate age and height, his colour and sex.

Now, before you start being critical, find something nice to say about him. Sometimes, when you have found the horse difficult, this can be hard, but it is always possible.

(b) Paces

Be realistic, neither over-flattering nor too damning. Say which pace you thought was the best and try to be quite clear in your description, e.g. 'the paces are round and rhythmic but tend to be a little short'.

(c) Rhythm
The horse may be rhythmic in all paces or rhythmic in only one or two and very erratic in the third. Try to link any lack of rhythm with a reason for this, e.g. the unrhythmic horse in walk is frequently a tense horse.

(d) Suppleness
Say which side the horse is stiff on. Mention the evasion or resistances he makes on this rein. Talk about any longitudinal stiffness and how it affects the horse's work.

(e) Balance
Your comments must relate to the stage of training of the horse – the novice horse will be working somewhat on his forehand, the elementary horse a little less so, but he cannot be expected to show the engagement of the quarters and the lightness of the forehand of the advanced horse. Again try to relate any loss of balance to the cause (e.g. the laterally stiff horse will become unbalanced when working on smaller circles and particularly in canter).

(f) Temperament
Include this point in your assessment as it obviously has a very direct bearing on the way the horse works and his training problems. Be careful not to be too harsh about a horse you find difficult to ride: it may be lack of feel or experience on your part rather than a lack of generosity on the part of the horse.

The paces

Walk

Four-time. The four beats must be evenly spaced or the walk becomes two-time. Important to keep checking that the walk is not deteriorating as the training advances. Few advanced dressage horses retain a really true four-time walk. Riders sometimes tend not to allow the horse to walk for periods between trot and canter work when schooling. Many novice horses have their walk hurried in an attempt to make the walk 'more active'.

Trot

Two-time. Care must be taken to establish the rhythm best suited to each particular horse. If taken too fast he will take short flat steps and appear to run. If too slow he may develop false elevation in his steps, which become unlevel and he appears to hover or 'swim'. Riders can tend to hurry short-striding horses in an effort to produce a rounder, more expressive trot. With the long-striding horse, the rider may tend to slow the rhythm too much as the horse with a naturally long stride can sometimes feel as if he is running away from the rider.

Canter

Three-time. Care must be taken not to make a young horse canter too slowly or ask for collection too soon or the canter will become 'broken' rather than three-time, and ultimately the four-time canter, common to many show jumpers, will appear.

Lateral work

The benefit to the horse

1. Improves obedience to the aids.
2. Supples the horse throughout his body.
3. Improves the horse's balance and so makes him more mobile through the shoulders (by lightening the forehand).
4. By activating the three joints of the hind leg, it improves the quality of the paces and they become softer and rounder.
5. By gaining better control of the quarters and shoulders it straightens the horse.
6. By developing and increasing the engagement of the hindquarters of the horse it improves the horse's ability to collect.

Aims

1. The horse must move forwards and sideways with correct bend (beware of too much neck bend).
2. The movement must be fluent, i.e. the rhythm and length of stride remains the same.
3. The horse's impulsion must be maintained and lateral work should be interspersed with periods of energetic forward work (e.g. lengthening of stride) to maintain or increase impulsion.
4. The outline of the horse must remain the same.

Turn on the forehand

This movement is only used to teach the horse the basic concept of moving forwards and sideways, in response to one leg, when hitherto he has learnt only to move forwards from both rider's legs. Once understood, this lesson is best left alone as the horse may quickly learn to swing his quarters before coming to halt if turn-abouts are ridden too frequently. It is also easy for the horse to drop behind the rider's leg and step backwards – a serious fault. A useful practical application of the movement is when opening gates.

It may be ridden anywhere in the school. The walk is slowed for two or three steps and the rider asks for a bend around his inside leg. The outside rein prevents the horse gaining ground too much to the front whilst the inside leg asks the horse to cross his inside hind leg in front of his outside hind leg. The outside foreleg should move forward round the inside foreleg. The horse thus turns about his forehand in a half turn of 180°. He must immediately be taken forwards on a straight line in walk or trot to restore the impulsion.

Common faults

1. Loss of bend.
2. The horse hollows.
3. The rider hurries the horse bringing the inside hind to the side of the outside hind foot with no crossing.
4. The rider fails to ride forwards soon enough out of the movement and the horse loses impulsion.

Leg yielding

Used as a preparation for shoulder-in by some people. Disliked and never taught by others who believe it encourages the horse to run away from the inside leg and escape through the outside shoulder. Useful when either horse or rider is inexperienced and therefore would find shoulder-in too demanding. Useful when working young or immature and rather weak horses for whom shoulder-in would be physically too demanding (too much strain on back and joints of hind leg for some four-year-olds.)

The horse moves on two tracks with a very slight bend at the poll away from the direction of the movement. He remains straight throughout his body. Done first in walk and then out of working trot (because there is virtually no bend, no collection is necessary – thus a useful exercise for a young horse).

Uses

1. Teaches a horse obedience to the diagonal aids.
2. Teaches the rider to co-ordinate the diagonal aids.
3. By encouraging the horse to step a little further under with his inside hind leg, makes him use the joints of his hind leg and so gives the working trot more softness and spring.
4. Makes the stiff horse more obedient to the rider's inside leg through turns and circles, which will help to supple him.

Once the movement can be performed correctly and easily, shoulder-in, which is of greater benefit, should be taught and ridden.

Aids

The inside leg asks the horse to move forwards and to the side. The outside leg helps to prevent the horse from stepping too much sideways and swinging his quarters. The inside rein asks for a very slight bend at the poll away from the direction the horse is moving. The outside rein prevents the horse from becoming crooked by escaping through his outside shoulder, whilst also controlling the speed of the pace.

Where ridden

1. *Line to line.* The horse is taken from one straight line to another, say from quarter line to inner track or centre line to quarter line, his body remaining parallel to the line. On reaching the second line he must be ridden positively forwards from the outside leg down the new line so that he goes forwards obediently out of the movement and does not learn to run sideways from the inside leg, escaping through the outside shoulder and so becoming crooked.

2. *Along the line.* Ridden at a very small angle (no more than 30°) but differing from shoulder-in because the horse has no bend in his body and the movement can and should be ridden in a working trot.

3. *Across the diagonal.* The horse is taken on to the diagonal line between opposite corner markers as if to change the rein across the diagonal. Then by clear half halts his body is brought parallel to the long side and he leg yields across the diagonal.

Shoulder-in

A lateral movement with the horse bent away from the direction of the movement. Can be on three or four tracks. The horse should be at an angle of no more than 30° to the wall. The space between the inside hind and outside fore must be no greater than that between the front and hind legs.

The benefit to the horse

1. Suppling.

2. Straightening (by gaining control of the shoulder).

3. Engages the quarters (so developing collection).

4. Useful preparation for other movements.

Aids

The inside rein leads the horse into the movement, supported by the outside rein. The inside leg maintains the impulsion and drives the horse forwards along the line of the movement. The outside leg behind the girth prevents the quarters from swinging out.

Where ridden

To be performed correctly the horse must be capable of some degree of collection in trot. This can initially be achieved by riding into the shoulder-in from a 10m circle. Later the horse will move into collected trot in response to the half halt.

Usually ridden from a 10m circle up the long side but can also be performed up the quarter line or centre line. May be ridden out of in the following ways:

1. Across the school on a curve.
2. On to a 10m circle.
3. Riding on to a diagonal line.
4. Straightening the horse and riding forward along the track.

The way in which the rider chooses to ride out of the movement will depend on the way in which the horse performs the movement, e.g:

1. Across the school on a curve used when the horse is learning the movement and is asked only for a few steps and then ridden forwards on a curve to prevent loss of impulsion, rhythm or bend.
2. On to a 10m circle when the horse begins to lose the bend.
3. Riding on to a diagonal line when using shoulder-in to develop lengthening of the stride.
4. Straightening the horse back to the track when the horse is tending to fall into the rider's inside leg and losing position.

The movement can initially be taught in walk, but it is very easy in this pace for the horse to drop behind the rider's leg so should never be done for long in walk. The movement is strenuous for a young or green horse and should not be sustained for long to begin with. A few correct steps are more beneficial than forcing the horse to move the whole length of the long side in a deteriorating shoulder-in.

Common faults

1. Forehand not sufficiently off track.
2. Too much neck bend.
3. Falling out through outside shoulder.
4. Pushing quarters out (rather than bringing forehand in).

5. Losing rhythm.
6. Losing impulsion.
7. Not equal on both reins.

Demi-pirouette

A useful preparation for travers and half pass. Demanded in medium tests. In walk the horse describes a turn of 180° moving his forehand around his quarters. The advanced horse makes canter pirouettes of 360°. The horse must make the smallest possible half circle without losing the rhythm of the walk, the impulsion or the bend. The horse is bent in the direction in which he is moving. The outside hind steps around the inside hind whilst the inside hind marks time on the spot. The walk rhythm must be maintained and he must not pivot on his inside hind. The front feet must cross one in front of the other. It is a very difficult movement for the rider to feel and help from the ground is usually necessary when either or both horse and rider are learning the movement.

Aids

The inside rein leads the horse into the movement, supported by the outside rein which also controls the amount of forward movement and bend the horse takes. The inside leg maintains the rhythm and impulsion of the walk. The outside leg prevents the quarters swinging.

Where ridden

In dressage tests it is asked for either along the long side or on a line across the school parallel to the E-B line. Preparation for demi-pirouette can be made by riding quarter turns, i.e. the 'Diamond' exercise. Ride on a straight line from one tangent point of a 20m circle to another and instead of turning through 90° by curving the horse, keep him straight so that he moves on to the next tangent point, each turn being a quarter pirouette.

Benefit to horse and rider

1. Improves collection by engaging inside hind leg.
2. Improves mobility of shoulders by gaining control of outside shoulder.

3. Improves turning and ability to ride out of a lateral movement.
4. Improves suppleness.
5. Improves rider's concentration and feel.

Common faults

1. Insufficient preparation before the movement, usually insufficient collection in the walk.
2. Insufficient bend.
3. The horse hollows.
4. Stepping backwards.
5. Losing walk sequence of footfalls.
6. Pivoting on inside hind.
7. Too large a circle.

Travers or quarters-in

Travers is disliked by some people who believe that since most horses have a natural inclination to make themselves crooked by pushing their quarters inwards, travers is offered by some horses as an evasion. Others believe that it is a useful preparation for half pass because the wall helps horse and rider maintain position. Since travers is essentially half pass the aids are the same (see below) and the faults similar. Care must be taken when riding travers that the rider concentrates on riding forwards into the bend from the inside leg and only asks for the hind feet to come in as far as the inner track. If the quarters are brought in too far the hind legs may cross but the horse will lose the bend and forward movement and so the exercise becomes of no value.

Half pass

The horse moves on two tracks, bent in the direction in which he is moving, with head, neck and shoulders slightly in advance of the quarters. Outside legs cross in front of inside legs.

Aids

Begins, as with shoulder-in, by bringing the forehand in off the track with an inside bend. Inside rein maintains bend and direction. Outside leg behind girth moves horse sideways, inside leg keeps horse moving forwards into the bend. The outside rein controls the pace and the amount of neck bend. Rider must look in the direction of the movement.

Where ridden
Usually done from the centre line back to the track. Some people prefer to ask initially for half pass from one quarter marker to the opposite quarter marker across the diagonal line, thus asking the horse for less bend and less crossing of the legs but making it harder for the horse to lead with his quarters (a common and persistent evasion). Initially asked for in walk, but, like shoulder-in, never ridden for too long in this pace as the horse tends to drop behind the rider's leg. May be performed in trot or canter.

Common faults
1. Wrong or insufficient bend (shoulder leading).
2. Quarters leading.
3. Quarters trailing.
4. Loss of impulsion.
5. Altering rhythm.
6. Insufficient crossing.
7. Too much bend in neck and loss of freedom of inside shoulder.

Rein back

The horse steps back in almost diagonal pairs, in a balanced manner, remaining on the bit. It will help to keep him straight if you ask alongside the boards or between two poles laid 3 feet apart.

Aids
Both legs ask for forward movement but as both hands are kept closed the horse has little alternative but to step backwards. It is best asked for by making a transition to halt from an impulsive working trot and instead of relaxing the aid and allowing the horse to remain still, the aids for halt are kept applied until the horse understands and steps to the rear. Should the horse be reluctant or confused an assistant on the ground is valuable. As the horse is ridden into the halt the assistant, standing in front of

the horse, may lightly tap the horse on the chest with the whip, saying 'Back'.

Common faults

1. The quarters swing and the horse is crooked.
2. The rein back is not two-time (the legs must move almost in diagonal pairs).
3. The horse crouches and shuffles back.
4. The horse hollows and resists.
5. The horse doesn't move forwards immediately after the rein back.
6. The horse anticipates, tenses and runs back.

Counter canter

Once the horse can canter a 15m and preferably a 10m circle with correct bend and in a good rhythm and balance, then he is ready to learn counter canter. The difference between counter canter and wrong lead is that in counter canter the horse is very slightly bent over the leading leg. It is a good straightening exercise for a horse that is crooked in canter (i.e. tends to bring his quarters in). By maintaining the inside bend (on the outside of the turn or circle in counter canter) the rider gains more control of the shoulder and so makes it more difficult for the horse to deviate with his quarters. It is indirectly a suppling movement. By gaining control of the outside shoulder of the horse, the rider is able to prevent the horse stiffening himself by falling out through this shoulder. It is a very good exercise to make the rider sit straight, still and upright maintaining a clear canter aid.

Aids

The rider must sustain a clear canter aid or the horse may change leg or become disunited. It must be remembered that 'outside' and 'inside' refer to the outside and inside of the bend, not the outside or inside of the circle. Thus when a horse is in left counter canter, he will be on the right rein, but leading with the left leg and bent to the left. The rider's left leg, although it is on the outside of the turn or circle, is still called the inside leg because it is on the inside of the bend. The rider must sit towards the inside of the bend.

Where ridden

1. In a 3m loop away from the wall (disliked by some people as it is easy to lose the bend or for the horse to go on two tracks).
2. Make a 15m half circle and return to the track before the corner marker. (Again disliked by some as the return to the track on this line makes it easy for the horse to lose rhythm and balance.)
3. Make a 10m half circle and return to the track between the centre marker and the corner marker. This demands that the horse is more supple and balanced in the canter before the counter canter is asked for, as he has to have the ability to canter a 10m half circle, but the return to the track is shorter and the horse is less likely to hurry and become unbalanced.
4. Take the horse in trot down the threequarter line of the school. Ask for counter canter strike off as the horse returns to the track and hold the counter canter for as long as the horse is capable.

Work on counter canter must be slowly progressive. Once the horse becomes excited or confused in this work it can develop into a longstanding problem. Until the horse is absolutely confident enough to remain in counter canter on 20m circles and large around the school, flying changes should not be attempted. Initially it is best not to ask the horse to go too deeply into the corners in counter canter. Once he can go around the short side of the school in counter canter take him across the diagonal line and change the rein, so rewarding him for his obedience by bringing him back to working canter on the new rein. If the horse changes leg, disunites or breaks the counter canter, he should be brought back to trot and asked immediately to strike off in counter canter lead to make it quite clear that he has been disobedient.

Shortening and lengthening the horse's paces

Once the horse is working on the bit in the basic paces, he may be asked to begin shortening and lengthening his steps. Begin first by asking for some shorter steps of trot. He can only show some correct lengthened strides once he has mastered shortening his steps to some degree. This is because without some engagement of the hindquarters (stepping further underneath his body with his hind legs) and a corresponding lightening of the forehand, he will not be in sufficiently good balance nor will he have sufficient stored-up impulsion to release to perform even some modest steps of lengthening (i.e. with the horse working well from behind in the same rhythm and outline as the working pace). It is important to work the horse equally in shortening and lengthening and not to develop one at the expense of the other.

Most horses will find one or other easier, depending on their conformation and natural movement. The forward-thinking, free-moving thoroughbred horse will find the extended trot less of a problem than the collected work (particularly if he has been bred for speed, with his hind leg set well back). The short-coupled cold-blooded horse with powerful quarters is likely to find the collected paces easier than the extended ones.

Shortening the stride

The horse will first learn to shorten his steps by making smaller circles. If he is ridden on a true 10m circle and he maintains a correct rhythm and bend and is working well on the bit and with the impulsion maintained, the circle will ensure that the steps of the horse become shorter and more elevated. Collection imposes quite a strain on the horse's back, stifles and hocks, so it must be sustained for only short periods to begin with. He should then be ridden forwards out of the collected trot into a good active working trot to prevent any tendency to lose impulsion and so drop behind the rider's leg and take tight, flat strides. The shortened steps must be rounder and higher as well as shorter.

When the horse is able to perform a correct 10m circle in trot he can be taught shoulder-in. The shoulder-in movement, by making the horse step further under his body with his inside leg, will improve and develop the horse's ability to collect in all paces. The horse will slowly learn obedience to the half halt, initially given before riding the small circle preceding shoulder-in and then in isolation as a signal to shorten his steps, i.e. to move from the working pace to the collected pace. The rider must always feel when asking for the collected pace that he is sending his horse from his legs up into his hand which restrains the increased impulsion from escaping in speed and channels it into shorter, higher steps. He must beware of any tendency to slow the horse down from the front, so producing a flat lifeless trot.

The aims of collection

1. Improves the horse's balance. (Some of the horse's natural balance is disturbed by the presence of a weight on his back.)
2. By developing the horse's ability to lower and engage his hindquarters, he will become lighter on his forehand and so more mobile in his shoulders.
3. His muscles will be developed in the right places and so his appearance will become more beautiful.
4. He will become a lighter and more responsive ride.

Lengthening the stride

Once the horse has learnt to collect to some degree, albeit only very modestly initially, he can be asked to lengthen his steps because the horse has some extra energy stored or restrained within the hindquarters to release into longer strides. It is best to ask initially either when coming from a 15 or 10m circle or after passing through a corner, ridden as deeply as the horse's stage of training will allow. Young horses will produce many evasions and resistances when asked to lengthen. They usually result from either lack of balance, lack of impulsion or crookedness, or a mixture of all three. He may run with short hurried steps, he may break into canter from trot, he may go wide behind, he may flick his toes out but fail to lengthen his stride behind, or he may hollow and become unsteady in his mouth. His steps may become uneven through lack of balance or crookedness. Do not be too ambitious in either the number of lengthened strides or the amount of lengthening the horse shows to begin with. Three strides, where the horse remains in the same rhythm, balance and outline are sufficient and the horse will form good habits rather than the reverse.

Some very stuffy not very forward-thinking horses, perhaps with certain conformation problems (e.g. straight shoulder or croup high) can be difficult to train in this work. Patience and perseverance are required. Almost any horse can be trained to produce a workmanlike medium trot and canter, though true extension may be outside their scope. Stimulating the horse either by an exciting environment (a windy day on the beach) or the company of other horses (a short sharp burst across an unfamiliar field with two or three other horses, followed by a request to lengthen the stride in the trot immediately afterwards) can sometimes be more effective than hours of nagging within a familiar schooling area.

Again, working on the principle that you can only lengthen a horse as much as you can shorten him, it is often a good idea to ask for the lengthening out of leg yielding in a young horse or shoulder-in from a more trained horse. In either case the rider must ask for the lengthened strides by sitting a little deeper and closing both legs simultaneously thus riding the horse up to a containing and supporting contact.

How strongly the aids are applied depends on the individual horse and his stage of training. The more advanced horse will take a more positive contact in medium trot, because he is in better balance and more full of impulsion. In any event, whether the horse is just learning to lengthen his stride or is capable of extension the same essentials apply:

1. The horse must be straight and in balance.
2. The rhythm remains the same, only the length of the steps alters.
3. The pace must be regular (i.e. no unlevel steps).
4. The horse must alter his stride equally behind and in front.
5. The horse's neck becomes a little longer and his face slightly more in front of the vertical.

Glossary of flatwork terms

BALANCE: The natural balance of the horse will, to some degree, be disturbed by the weight of the rider. By training the horse progressively he will develop the ability to lower and engage his hindquarters further underneath his body thus lightening and freeing his forehand.

BEHIND THE LEG: The horse is more or less inattentive to the leg. He may break into another pace or he may remain in the same pace but he is neither mentally nor physically going forwards from the pressure of the leg into the contact of the hand.

CADENCE: Roundness and softness of the steps, making the paces expressive. Cadence may be inherent in the horse's paces or it may be developed to some degree through training.

ENGAGED BEHIND (COLLECTION): Varies in degree according to the horse's stage of training. The horse steps well underneath his body with his hind legs bent and supple.

EVASION: A means by which the horse avoids entirely or partially carrying out the request of his rider.

HALF HALT: An almost invisible and simultaneous signal from the rider, using legs, seat and hand to increase horse's attention and improve his balance before entering an exercise or transition.

IMPULSION: Energy stored or generating from the hindquarters. A forward urge.

ON THE BIT: The horse's hocks are correctly placed, he is rounded over his topline, with the neck more or less raised and arched according to the stage of training and the pace in which he is working. He accepts the bit with a steady even contact. The poll must be the highest point. The horse offers no resistance to the rider.

ON THE LEG (ON THE AIDS): The horse is obedient and attentive to the rider's leg and hand aids (i.e. neither behind the leg nor running away from it). Not to be confused with the expression 'on the leg' meaning a long-legged, rather weak horse showing a lot of daylight beneath his body.

OUTLINE: The shape in which the horse is working. The horse may take a rounded outline but may not be working on the bit (e.g. he has dropped the contact or he is stiff in his back and resistant in his mouth).

RESISTANCE: The horse displays tension and an unwillingness to submit to the rider's request.

RHYTHM: The regularity of the footfalls.

SUBMISSION: The horse's obedience, manifested by a willing, confident attitude and a lightness and harmony in his work.

TEMPO: The speed of the rhythm.

VOLTE: A 6m circle.

Movements required at various levels

Preliminary – Tests 1–8

Halt sustained for 4 seconds.
Working paces on both reins. All trot work may be done rising or sitting.
20m circles in trot and canter
Half 10m circles in walk and trot.
Lengthened strides in trot.
All transitions may be progressive.

Novice – Tests 12–19

As above and:
6m circle in walk.
Serpentine loops in trot.
Reins in one hand in trot.
Give and retake the reins in trot and canter.
15m circles in trot.
15m and 10m half circles in canter.
A few strides counter canter.
Canter from walk.
Lengthened strides in canter.
Change of rein in canter through trot.
Lengthened strides in canter.
Rein back three or four steps.

Elementary – Tests 22–29

Halt sustained for 6 seconds.
All trot work must be executed sitting.
Transitions may be progressive unless stated otherwise.
Variations within the pace in walk, trot and canter.
10m circles in trot.
Shoulder-in.
15m circles in canter.

4.

JUMPING

Gymnastic jumping

A system of training the horse to jump by dictating and controlling his position of take-off at each fence. This is done either by a placing pole on the ground a measured distance from the fence, or by a series of trotting poles in front of the fence or by another smaller fence in front of a larger fence. This concept is then built up in the form of a line of fences, known as a grid. Each element of the grid is a carefully measured distance from the next element, ensuring that the horse is brought to a good, safe position to take off, helping the horse to round or bascule over his fences. By altering the distances between the ground poles and the fences, the horse learns to lengthen and shorten his stride coming in to his fences and begins to develop his own 'eye for a stride' – a very valuable asset to most riders who will never become absolutely accurate in their judgement of pace and distance on the approach to fences.

Whilst useful to develop confidence and technique of both horse and rider gymnastic jumping can be overused, so that horse and rider become too dependent on being placed at every fence by poles and placing fences, and never develop their own initiative and feel on the approach to a fence. Gymnastic jumping should be regarded as a means to an end rather than as an end in itself. After performing a gymnastic jumping exercise, horse and rider should jump a suitable and unrelated fence to find out whether the exercise has been helpful and effective.

Objects

1. To give the horse a good jumping style.
2. To make the horse bold and develop his initiative.
3. To make the horse as athletic as possible.
4. To make the horse easier to ride by getting him going freely and calmly.
5. Gives the rider the opportunity to concentrate on himself and so improve his own technique.
6. Improves rider's balance, suppleness and grip.

Style

The horse must approach the fence confidently and calmly. He must be in a good rhythm and length of stride and in the best balance possible, dependent on his stage of training. He must be straight in front of the fence and have sufficient impulsion for the fence to be jumped. To take off, he must lower a little behind and spring off his hocks. In the air, his front legs must fold up well in front of his elbows. His hind legs should also be neatly folded and he should push them slightly behind his body as he descends. By lowering and stretching his neck he gives the impression of rounding his back. He must land quietly and continue straight, regaining his balance and rhythm almost immediately. The jump should appear smooth and fluent with a minimum of effort.

Common faults

1. Loss of rhythm in front of the fence. Either the horse tries to hurry (sometimes anxiety, sometimes habit), or he drops behind the rider's leg and drops the contact, so losing rhythm and impulsion.
2. The horse is unbalanced approaching the fence, often as a result of stiffness through a corner.
3. The horse becomes hollow and fights the contact on the approach.
4. Becomes crooked by swinging his quarters and approaches the fence in a crab-like manner (usually due to anticipation of the jump and anxiety).
5. Insufficient impulsion (the horse is mentally hanging back or inattentive).
6. The horse jumps flat and across the fence.

7. The legs are not equally folded (one or both of a pair dangles).
8. The horse does not jump the centre of the fence but hangs to left or right.
9. The horse jumps 'in two halves'.
10. The horse 'dwells' or hovers in the air (often greenness).
11. The horse 'explodes' on landing and tries to take charge.

Whilst it is true that some horses have more natural aptitude to jump than others, the faults outlined above are most often the result of poor riding. Rider problems will be discussed in the teaching notes which follow this section.

Ways of placing a horse in a good position to take off

1. Single pole on the ground, preferably a square one which is less likely to roll if trodden on. Placed usually 9-10 ft from the fence, which may be an upright or a spread. Occasionally 8ft may be used with a horse with some natural athleticism to make him back off the fence and use himself better. Initially 11-12ft can also be used with big, long-striding horses. There is the danger that a bold horse will attempt to jump the pole and fence in one, so careful introduction is needed. Helps the horse to take off in the correct place and off a short 'platform'. By varying the distance between the pole and the jump he can be brought deeper or further away from the fence to take off, so teaching him to be adaptable in emergencies.
2. Trotting poles. Placed between 4-6ft apart, depending on the horse's stride. Usually 9-10ft from the last pole to the fence. Has a relaxing and calming influence on horse and rider and should improve the rhythm on the approach. The horse must be working well over the poles before the fence is introduced.
3. Placing fence, a safer method than the single pole on the ground. Can be jumped out of trot or canter but out of trot will make the horse use himself more over the second fence. Placing fence should be 2ft – 2ft 6ins high, set 18-21 ft away from the second fence. Occasionally with a very big, long-striding youngster the distance may be longer at first. The placing fence is a valuable exercise for novice horses and/or riders. It makes them meet the fence at a good place to take off so that the jump itself should be a good one thus

building up confidence and boldness. It teaches the horse to cope with more difficult distances and is an introduction to jumping combination fences (i.e. doubles and trebles). It encourages stuffy horses to be more freegoing.

4. Series of fences (a grid). Usually jumped from trot but may be out of canter with backward-thinking horse. Fences placed 18-24ft apart. Bounce strides of 9-10ft may be used. Builds up confidence in horse and rider and improves their athleticism. Distances between fences may be varied to suit individual horses and improve their technique.

Gymnastic exercises

1. Single pole

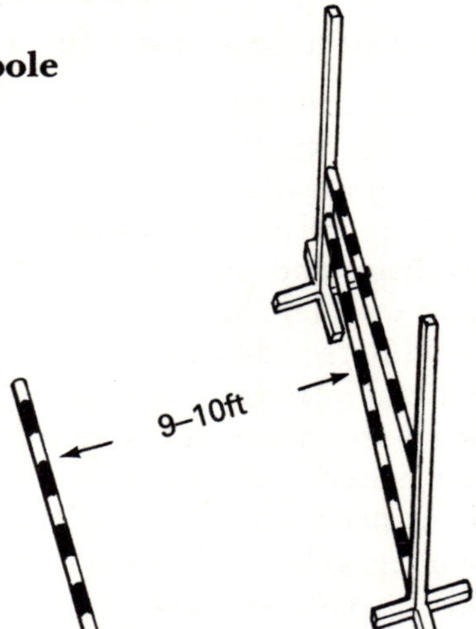

2. Trotting poles

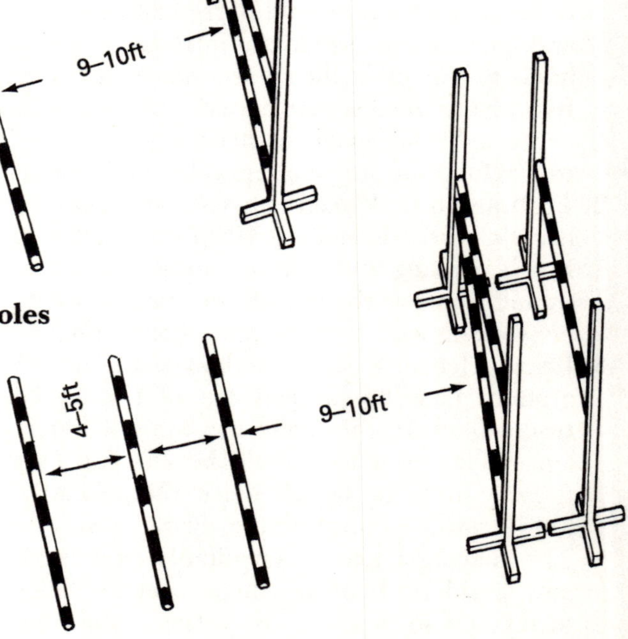

3. Placing fence

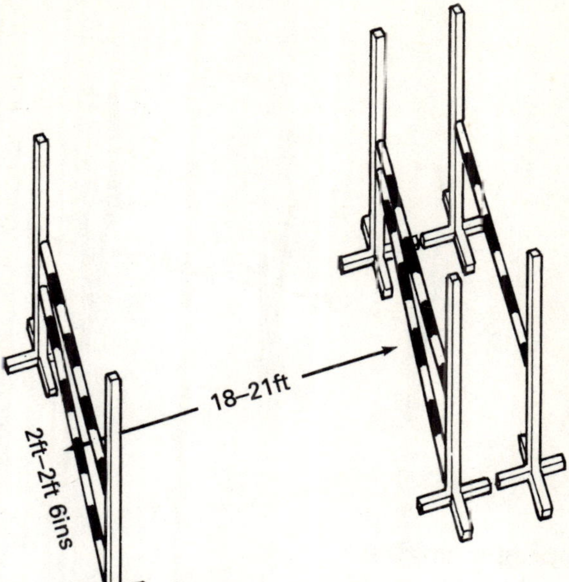

4. Trotting poles around a curve
Makes horse's hind legs more active.

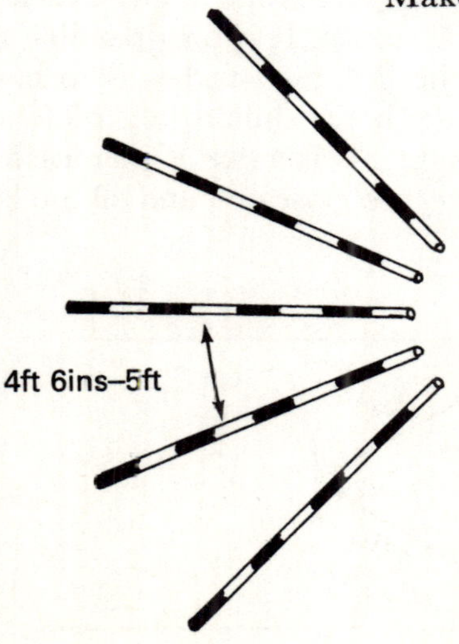

5. A grid (use as many variations as possible)

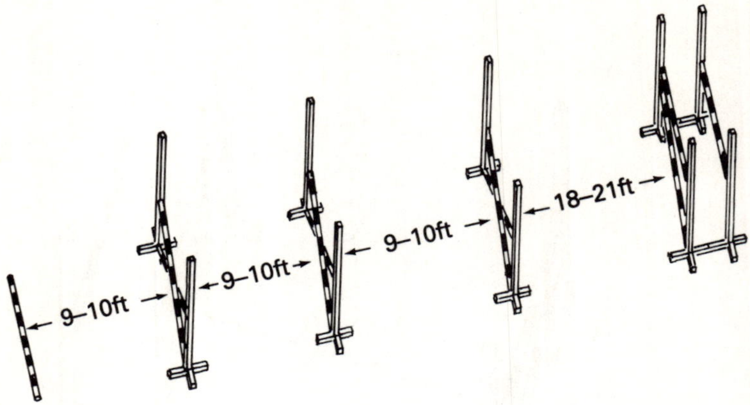

6. Jumping at angles

Teaches horse to bend and turn on landing and to shorten and lengthen his stride as he changes direction. Makes horse use himself over relatively small fences. Improves rider's use of the leg when making turns. Can be made progressively more difficult by moving A and B to form an increasing angle. Teaches horse and rider to become more accurate. It is also possible to make small adjustments within the last two strides as to how near or far away from the fence the horse should take off, (i.e. by veering slightly to the left or right). It is a useful exercise for horses that are inclined to either get too close or stand off too far from fences.

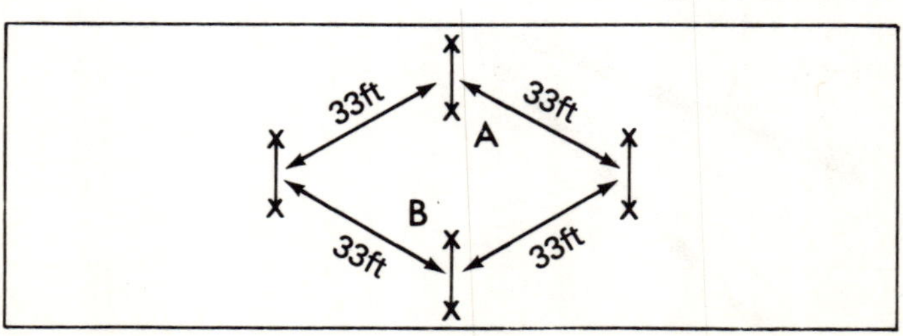

7. Teaching the horse to turn

Jump fence (a) and then (b), then change the rein and jump (a) and then (c). Jump equally on both reins. The wall or fence will assist in turning the horse By moving the three fences closer together the turns can be made tighter. Next progress to jumping either (b) or (c) and then (a) (no wall or fence to assist in turning).

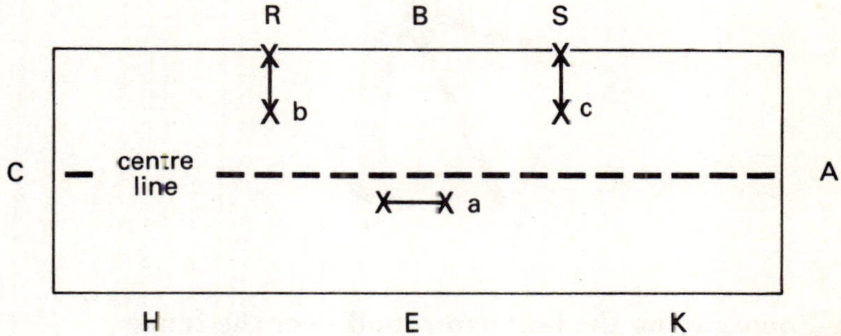

8. Teaching the horse to shorten or lengthen the stride

The horse works on a continuous figure of eight, trotting first over three trotting poles, taking a bounce stride to a cross pole followed by a short stride to a small upright. He then changes the rein and goes through an identical exercise but this time with a longer stride before the upright. He learns to develop an eye for distances in combination and an ability to lengthen and shorten between fences.

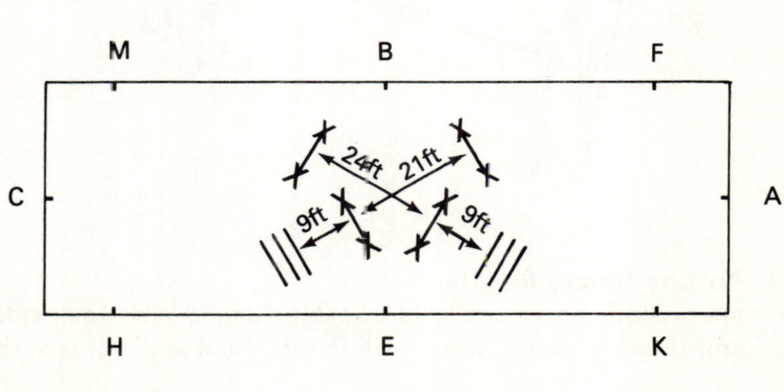

9. Leading the horse to the centre of the fence
Useful in correcting a horse which persistently jumps to one side of the fence.

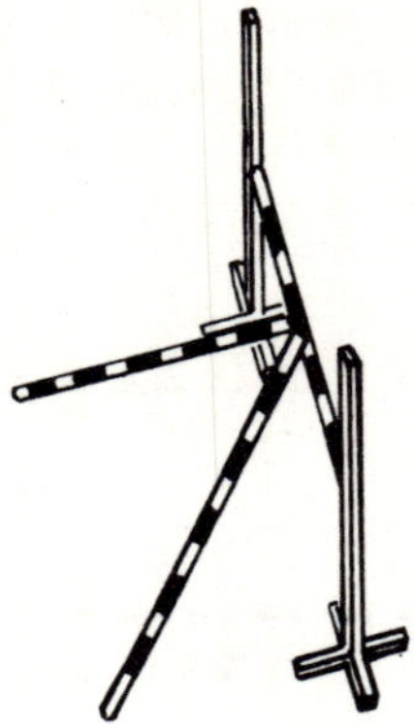

10. Encouraging the horse to round over the fence
Two low, but wide parallels with a short non-jumping stride of 18-22ft between them will encourage horse to look down, lower head and neck and use his back.

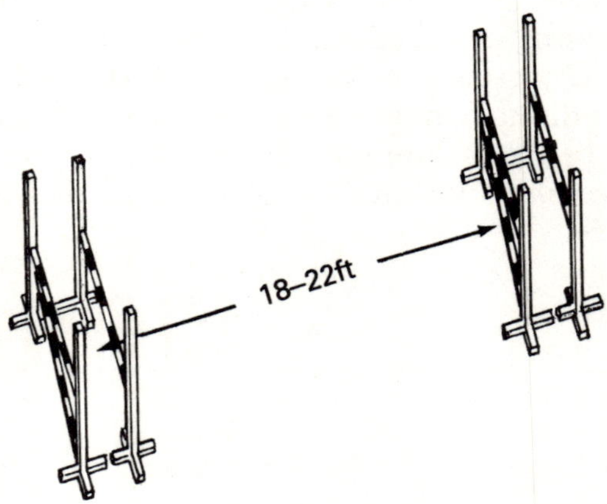

11. Putting fences together
A good preliminary exercise before asking a novice horse or rider to jump round a course. Start with fences small and trot into the

jumps. Then raise the fences and jump from canter. Encourages rider to ride forwards into the fences and asks the horse to jump out of his stride.

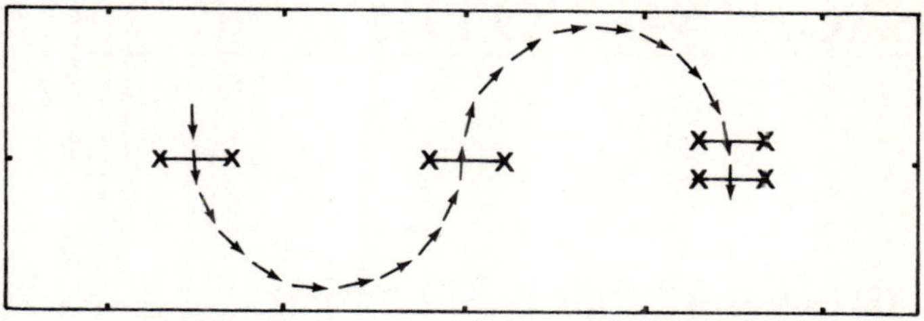

Once horse and rider have gained confidence and a sound technique through this type of work they are ready to begin jumping a small course.

Problems likely to occur when jumping a course for the first time

1. Horse becomes anxious, losing concentration, rhythm and balance.
2. Horse becomes over-excited and rushes his fences.
3. Horse spooks at one or several unfamiliar fences.
4. Horse is difficult to turn because he is insufficiently supple and obedient in his flatwork.

Most young and/or inexperienced horses will benefit by regular gymnastic jumping work alongside their competition work. Many experienced jumpers are helped by a return to simple gymnastic exercises to restore confidence when problems arise in the ring. Event horses, in particular, who have to be capable of negotiating very difficult distance problems in combination fences which, being solid, are very unforgiving of mistakes, need a very thorough grounding of gymnastic jumping.

5.

TEACHING NOTES

The flat lesson (approx. 30 mins.)

Horse working at Preliminary, Novice or Elementary level. You will be given a brief, including horse's age and experience, and some information about the rider, e.g. how much he has ridden the horse. Your brief may be very general, such as the horse is working towards a certain test in the future or the rider needs some help, or it may be specific, such as help this rider with counter canter. In any case, stick to the brief and try not to get sidetracked. Try to form a good rapport with the rider from the beginning (many people dislike guinea pigging). Be careful not to talk down to him. Try to be cheerful, helpful and calm in your manner (nervousness can have the effect of making you sound bored, tired or bossy). Have a quick look at the tack to see that there is nothing incorrectly fitted that will affect the horse's performance.

Begin by asking the rider to let you see the horse in walk, trot and canter on both reins and to show you any lateral work the horse is capable of and any lengthening of the stride the horse can make. Watch carefully, trying to decide where the problems lie and how to help the rider with them. Do not allow the rider to take too long over working in the horse; this should only last about five minutes.

Bring the rider in to the centre. Do not say too much at this stage, as you may change your mind a little or a lot after riding the horse. Ask if you can sit on the horse to feel how he goes and make some pleasant encouraging remark about what you have seen so far. This will help your rapport with your pupil once you begin the lesson proper. Be careful not to stay riding the horse too long (even if he proves either a very difficult ride or a very enjoyable one) or you will leave yourself short of teaching time. Do not attempt to school the horse. Ride him quietly on both reins in all three paces, ask him to shorten and lengthen his steps and find out how much lateral work he is capable of. Note his stiff side. If the horse goes less well for you than the rider do not worry unduly and neither criticise the horse harshly (it may be your lack of confidence, feel or experience) nor denigrate yourself by saying something like 'I'm sorry he went like a drain for me!' You are being examined as a teacher, not as a rider. It is a bonus if the horse goes well for you but not the end of your chances if he doesn't, so long as you don't lose your head and start riding tactlessly and aggressively. Try to find something nice to say about the horse and then tell the rider briefly where you think the problems lie both with the horse and rider and what you are going to work on to try and improve them. Always be sure when you are talking to the rider that you put yourself in a position where the examiner as well as the rider can hear you.

You should leave yourself with about twenty minutes in which to teach. Try to begin by working on the most basic problem you have noted (e.g. the horse is inattentive to the leg) and use exercises appropriate to the problem and to the horse's stage of training. If a particular exercise is not helping, then try to think of an alternative one rather than going on and on getting nowhere. Be careful to work on both reins equally and it is usually best to include work in all three paces. This should produce a more interesting, varied and enjoyable lesson than one spent entirely in, say, working trot. If horse and rider are not really up to the level at which you have been told to work in the brief, return to the basics rather than have the horse struggling to perform more difficult movements and doing them so badly the work is of no value.

Try to finish on a good note. Be encouraging even if the lesson has not gone as planned, but at the same time be realistic and do not over-praise. Leave the rider with a plan to work on until the next lesson.

N.B. Be careful of where you stand to teach. Do not walk around constantly, this is distracting to horse and rider. Try to be in front of the horse when watching lateral work as you will see the straightness of the horse and the angle at which he is working better.

The jumping lesson (approx. 20 mins.)

A set of fences will be laid out. You may alter them as you wish. Be guided by the brief as to what height you have them. If the horse is going to a riding club one-day event he will be jumping 3ft to 3ft 3ins, so apart from the first few warm-up jumps, which should always be low and encouraging, try to work with the fences about that height. Very low fences when the horse is used to and capable of jumping much bigger fences can be very misleading (he may jump carelessly or start rushing through lack of respect). On the other hand, be equally careful not to get carried away and over-face either or both horse and rider. When altering fences, or distances between them, try to handle the jumps quickly and efficiently. It is no good spending threequarters of the lesson building an elaborate grid and leaving yourself five minutes' teaching time. Be very, very careful that distances in combinations are suitable and therefore safe. Try to decide whether the horse's stride is long or short. If he is a long-striding horse, trotting poles should be 5 ft apart, a bounce 10ft and a non-jumping stride 21-24ft. If the horse is short striding, trotting poles will be 4ft 6ins apart, a bounce 9ft and one non-jumping stride 18-21ft.

Before starting the lesson, find out from the rider the horse's age and jumping experience (i.e. what competitions he has done), also whether the rider has ridden the horse often or rarely and how much competitive jumping they have done. This will give you some guide as to how ambitious you can be in setting up the fences or gymnastic exercises. Ask to see the horse in trot and canter and then jumping an upright, a spread and a combination fence, either out of trot or canter, whichever the rider prefers. If the rider chooses to canter over very small fences it is often a sign that the horse is rather idle or stuffy and this can give you a lead as to where the basic problem lies. You may well see many faults relating to the flatwork (e.g. the very stiff horse who loses his balance on turns). Mention it and, if possible, try to relate it to the jumping exercises you choose, but avoid turning the lesson into a flat lesson: you must work the horse and rider over fences.

After the rider has jumped these warm-up fences bring him in and tell him what you have seen. Try to be encouraging and avoid being over-critical. Try to decide what weakness or problems you are going to work on and choose a helpful exercise. Always try to finish by asking the rider to jump several fences together, hopefully to show that the chosen exercise has improved horse and rider's jumping. Be careful neither to talk too much and so distract the rider or make him flustered, nor, especially if the horse makes a bad approach or jump, to say nothing and hope that the next attempt will be better. Be quick and positive if things go wrong. If the horse stops, try to tell the rider immediately why and what to do when he re-presents the horse at the fence. If the horse stops a second time always make the fence easier and then build it up again once the horse is jumping confidently.

Typical problems

1. Nervous or inexperienced rider

If the horse is jumping badly and you are uncertain why, look at the rider's face on the approach and in the air. The rider may talk very confidently and appear knowledgeable and experienced on the flat but may be very apprehensive and therefore inhibiting to the horse when jumping. He may be worrying about one of two things – where and when the horse is going to take off and/or staying with the horse in the air. The latter is usually a subconscious fear and almost always relates to a weak jumping position. In the former case try to persuade the rider that his 'eye' will develop with experience and that he does not need to see a stride until the fences are much bigger (around 4ft). His job is to ride the horse into the fence straight, in good rhythm and balance, keeping the horse on a fairly short stride, and with sufficient impulsion for the horse to jump the fence easily out of his stride. Use a placing fence first of all in front of a vertical fence and then make the vertical into a spread. Make the distance between the two fences absolutely easy for the horse (between 18ft and 21ft). Try to follow up by asking the rider to jump a single unrelated fence after the jump with the placing fence. Hopefully they will be more confident and flowing and you can ask them to put several fences together.

2. Problems in turning
Usually a sign that the horse is laterally very stiff. You can explain that this problem really stems from the flatwork but do not turn the lesson into a flat lesson. Jumping one or two fences on a very large circle may help or, if suitable fences and time is available, use exercise 5, 6 or 11 from the previous section.

3. Rushing
Usually due to lack of acceptance of rider's leg on the flat. Mention this and use trotting poles in front of a small fence. If the horse rushes, remove the fence and ask the rider to circle in front of the poles, only allowing the horse to trot over the poles when he is calm and rhythmic. Then add the fence. Use very short approaches, so that the horse has less time to anticipate the jump. Walk jumping can be helpful but explain that this needs to be done regularly over a period of time before the horse loses the habit of rushing.

4. Stuffy horse (puts in extra strides and props)
Usually idle and inattentive to rider's leg on the flat. Ask the rider to make some acute transitions before jumping and to lengthen and shorten the canter. Use either a placing jump with a small fence behind (gradually lengthen the distance to make the horse jump more boldly and generously) or put two fences on a large circle to be jumped out of canter (makes rider ride forwards with legs into fence), or three fences in a line to be jumped through serpentine loops (exercise 11 from the previous section).

5. Jumping flat (no bascule over fence)
Usually related to the horse quickening and lengthening his stride on the approach. This often happens when the rider panics and overrides on the approach. It is also the result of the rider overchecking on the approach in an effort to find the take-off

stride for the horse. In this situation a brave horse will take hold of the bit and attempt to take charge of the situation himself. A placing pole on the ground in front of a cross pole 9ft away to a small true parallel 14-15 yards (three non-jumping strides) away will prove useful to contain the horse on the last three strides before the fence. The placing pole and cross fence to be jumped from trot.

The class lesson (approx. 20 mins.)

Usually four to six riders of about Stage II or III standard, mounted on school horses. Exam candidates work in pairs. One rides leading file and the other teaches, then they change places.

The lesson must be safe and sound at all times. Take into account the terrain, weather and standard of horses and riders. If you are outside on a cold windy day beware of 'leading file in succession' exercises, particularly in canter. Stirrups may be taken away in trot if the weather and the standard of horse and rider are suitable. Never have the ride cantering without stirrups. If the weather is very hot be careful not to work the ride so hard that horses and riders are steaming!

Show a variety of simple and easily understood exercises (avoid complicated or unusual exercises which may make ride control difficult). Be absolutely audible at all times (you may have to use a really strong voice outside on a windy day) but avoid shouting and/or an aggressive manner. Alternate exercises which the ride perform together with 'leading file in succession' exercises. The latter gives horse and rider a breather and gives the instructor the opportunity to concentrate on helping individuals. Try to improve the riders' positions and use of the aids whilst maintaining a well-disciplined and varied lesson. Speak slowly and avoid negative commands (e.g. 'Come upright' rather than 'Don't tip forwards'). Help all the riders equally: it is very easy, unintentionally, to concentrate on the most capable rider and/or a very weak rider. Avoid cantering all the ride together when the horses are unfamiliar to you – the unexpected and disastrous may occur. Be quick to praise and encourage any improvement shown, particularly from the weaker or less-experienced riders.

The lunge lesson (approx. 15 mins.)

The rider will be an 'improver', i.e. roughly stage III or better, and will have been lunged before. First lunge the horse to get the feel of him on both reins. Ask whether he has already been lunged in side reins and, if so, save time by attaching the side reins immediately. This, of course, may not be possible if you are the first candidate to lunge in this section and you will have to lunge without the side reins first. Make sure you put the horse on to a good-sized circle (about 15m) and that he is obedient to your voice in the transitions. Be quiet but positive with the stodgy horse. Wake him up and make him move forwards from the whip in a proper working trot, not the steady, economical jog you would want with a beginner rider having their first lunge lesson. When you feel you have the horse's attention and respect, get the rider mounted (first undo the side reins).

Common faults with the improver

1. Sits crooked (collapses inside hip).
2. Twists (leads with one shoulder).
3. Lacks balance (leans behind vertical or tips forwards off seat bones).
4. Stiff (may be an overall stiffness or in one specific place).
5. Lacks depth (draws up knees and grips with calves, toes out).

Be sure the rider in no way starts to ride the horse. He must sit still and allow you to control the horse. Begin in walk and trot allowing the rider use of reins and stirrups. Get a good picture of the rider's positional faults before you ask the rider if he is happy for you to take away the reins and stirrups. It is usually more effective to lunge this standard of rider without reins and stirrups but if the rider is weak or apprehensive it may not be possible, or at least not until towards the end of the lesson when you have made some improvement. If in any doubt about the horse's steadiness and reliability, do not take the reins and stirrups away. It is safer to stick to walk and trot if you do not know the horse well. However, if you know the horse has a really well-balanced canter and the rider is particularly capable, you may canter him for a short period, but not without stirrups.

Be pleasant but firm with the rider. Correcting positional faults on the lunge can be boring to some riders, so you have to hold their attention and be conscientious in maintaining any improvement you are able to make. Use transitions to walk, halt and trot to add variety and test the rider's balance and suppleness. Include any appropriate exercises but avoid doing exercises for their own sake when they are not relevant to the rider's problems. The more capable the rider, the more active you can make the horse's paces. If you take the rider's reins and stirrups away, always have him holding on to the front of the saddle to begin with. Only when you feel he is sufficiently well balanced should you allow him to let go of the saddle. If, when he does let go, he is unable to maintain a correct position and starts to grip up or stiffen, tell him to hold on again, at least with the outside hand.

Exercises

1. Drawing up knees and pushing them strongly down. Rids thigh and knee of tension.
2. Shoulder shrugging. Helps tension at back of neck and between shoulders.
3. Head rolling. Good follow-up to exercise 2 above.
4. Raising inside arm and pressing backwards three times. Correction for round shoulders.
5. Knees away from saddle (at walk only). Loosens hip joint and stretches thigh muscles.
6. Bending forwards to touch toe. Stretches back muscles, suppling.
7. Bending backwards (at halt only), supples spine.
8. Turning to the side, strengthens pelvis, abdomen and spine.

All exercises must be done slowly and the rider must not compensate by twisting or stiffening.

The lecturette (approx. 5 mins.)

You will be given your lecturette subject on a piece of paper and will usually have about 15 minutes to prepare it. Make a plan of what you are going to say. Avoid writing too much down as you must not read out notes. You must deliver the lecture as if to a group of students in a lecture room situation. Divide the content of your lecture under sub-headings, using a rough diagram to illustrate where appropriate. A blackboard will be available and it can be effective to use it.

For example:

Maintenance of paddocks

(a) **Reasons for** (safety, health of horse, worm control, obtaining best return from land).

(b) **Methods** (regular collection of droppings, chain harrowing, fertilising, resting, alternating cattle and horses, controlling weeds, maintaining fencing and water supply).

(c) **Equipment**

Your voice and delivery are very important. However good the content of your lecture, if your voice is monotonous, too quiet, or you speak too quickly and run one sentence into the next, you will be difficult to follow. Allow plenty of light and shade in your voice, emphasise important points by speaking slowly and pause before you go on to the next point. Finish your lecture by asking if anyone has any questions. Try to have a good opening and closing sentence memorised.

If you find giving a lecturette difficult the following suggestions may help improve your confidence.

1. Borrow a tape recorder and record your lecturette on to a tape and play it back. You may be rather disconcerted by your first attempt but if you persevere you will quickly notice an improvement. This is particularly useful if you tend to repeat yourself or use one word or phrase to link each and every sentence. It is also an effective way of making you realise how many times you 'um' and 'er' between sentences. You will then begin to deliver the lecturettes more fluently.

2. Practise using a blackboard. One will be supplied in the exam. With some subjects, it works very well to write your plan of the subject on the board either before starting the talk or as you go along. Using the blackboard makes you stick to a plan and avoids repetition.

3. Using the following list of subjects as a guide, make plans of several or all of the subjects on cards.

Possible subjects for the lecturette

1. Explain to a new working pupil the daily routine and timetable in your yard.

2. On her first morning with you, explain to your newly qualified BHSAI what her duties will be and how many horses she will have to look after.

3. How many horses should (a) your working pupil look after and (b) your paid groom look after?

4. Give your ideas on what your responsibilities are to your working pupils and what they may expect of you as an employer.

5. Stable construction – what you like and dislike.

6. Stable fittings and ventilation.

7. Watering systems.

8. Organisation of your tack room.

9. Efficient organisation of work in the yard.

10. Organisation of the feed room.

11. Labour-saving arrangements around the yard and in the stable.

12. The care of ponies at grass (a) in the summer and (b) in the winter.

13. Necessary equipment needed for the efficient running of a yard of twenty horses.

14. Instructions to staff on receiving a livery.

15. Instructions to junior staff on procedure to be followed when a livery leaves the yard.

16. Maintenance of an outdoor school surface.

17. Safety measures in and around the yard.
18. What must be done in freezing weather.
19. Instructions to staff on taking a hack.
20. Instructions to staff on checking a ride. With riders new to them, what information do they need?
21. Safety precautions when mounting your ride – what to check with regard to the rider and the horse.
22. The reception and care of riding clients.
23. Procedure in event of an accident to a rider on a hack or in the school.
24. A horse goes lame on a hack – instruct junior staff what to do.
25. Fire drill.
26. Fire precautions in the yard and stables.
27. Spring-cleaning.
28. The care and storage of rugs and unused saddlery.
29. Clipping a difficult horse – procedure and precautions to be taken.
30. Different types of clip and when to use them.
31. Maintenance of electric clippers.
32. Strapping – the theory and importance of good grooming.
33. Describe different types of corrective shoeing in general use and under what circumstances they should be used.
34. What to look for in the well-shod horse and some common shoeing faults.
35. Grassland management.
36. Insurance.
37. The Road Safety Test.
38. Principles of watering.
39. The importance of water to the horse and occasions when it should be withheld.
40. Instruct junior staff when they should call the vet in your absence.
41. The practical points relevant to the diet of a horse.
42. Common disorders and problems caused by incorrect feeding.
43. The administration of medicines.
44. Dealing with minor cuts, abrasions and bruising.
45. Reasons for poulticing the foot and methods.
46. Care of the hunter (a) the morning of the hunt and (b) after hunting.

47. Methods of controlling bleeding.
48. Basic structure of the foot.
49. Give reasons and methods of fomenting, hosing and tubbing.
50. Diagnosis of lameness.
51. The reasons for variation of diet between different horses in the yard.
52. The rules of feeding.
53. Duties of an assistant manager (head boy or head girl) on a yard.
54. Organisation of daily routine and yard timetable.
55. How to ensure health and soundness in working horses.
56. Calculating the diet requirements for a yard of horses.
57. How to work out training programmes for novice one-day event horses and long-distance horses.
58. Maintenance of facilities.
59. Symptoms of lameness.

Possible subjects for discussion

After giving your lecturette, you will take part in a discussion with the examiner and other candidates. It is likely that topics covered will include subjects relating to office management and organisation of rides.

1. How do you organise the booking of rides?
2. How do you allocate horses?
3. What system do you have for assessing rides before assigning them to a group or class?
4. What arrangements do you make for clients to pay?
5. Do you recommend a system of a course of lessons at a reduced fee?
6. What is a filing system?
7. What equipment and books are necessary in a well-organised office?
8. What records should you keep in relation to your horses?
9. Why should you keep an accident/incident book?
10. Explain your system of keeping accounts.
11. Insurance: What is (a) compulsory, (b) advisable, (c) debatable?
12. What is involved in applying for BHS approval?

13. Why should every horse owner be a member of the BHS?
14. What information does your accountant require from you when preparing your end of year accounts?
15. Freeze-marking horses – why and what is involved?
16. Marking of saddlery for identification.
17. Prices of (a) lessons and rides, (b) stabled livery, (c) grass livery.

6.

COMPETITIONS

A good instructor needs to be familiar with and reasonably up to date on the rules for various competitions. There is no need to be a walking rulebook, but it is helpful to be able to guide pupils towards competitions for which they are eligible and which will be within their capabilities and those of their horse. Rules change, often on a yearly basis, so it is always as well to check in the appropriate current rulebook.

Dressage

For affiliated competitions a rider must be a member of the BHS and also a member of the Dressage Group. Horses must be four years old. There is no lower height limit, i.e. ponies may be ridden. Horses must be registered with the Dressage Group and will be issued with a registration number which must be given on all competition entries. Horses may, however, enter Preliminary classes without being registered, since no grading points are awarded. Horses are graded according to the number of points won: 7 points are awarded for first place, 6 for second, and so on to 1 point for seventh place.

Grading

NOVICE – less than 50 points.
ELEMENTARY – less than 100 points.
MEDIUM – less than 200 points.
ADVANCED – 250 points upwards.

All tests up to Prix St Georges may be commanded. Snaffles only are permitted for Novice tests; snaffles or double bridles for Elementary and Medium; double bridles for Advanced. No boots, bandages or martingales are allowed. Cavesson, drop or flash nosebands with snaffles are permitted (grakles may be worn in horse trials). Spurs may be used in all tests and are compulsory in Medium classes upwards. Whips are permitted at all levels.

Show jumping

For affiliated competitions, owners and riders must be full members of the BSJA and the horse must be registered. Horses are graded according to amount of prize-money won.

Seniors

GRADE C – less than £450, also includes Newcomers for horses having won less than £30. Fences 3ft 3ins – 3ft 6ins in first round, 3ft 10ins in jump-off, including one double of uprights and no water jump. Foxhunter, for horses having won less than £300 with fences 3ft 9ins in the first round and 4ft 1in. in the jump-off. Winners of Newcomer and Foxhunter competitions qualify for regional finals and then a final.

GRADE B – less than £1000.

GRADE A – £1000 and over.

Juniors

Ponies must be registered with the BSJA and not exceed 14.2hh, holding a life height certificate. There are three grades:

JD – ponies having won less than £20.
JC – ponies having won less than £300.
JA – ponies having won £300 or more.

Competitions include:

Junior Badminton, also open to unregistered ponies as well as JD – maximum height: 2ft 6ins.

Junior Newcomers, open to JD and JC having won less than £50 – maximum height: 3ft.

Junior Foxhunter, ponies having won less than £150 – maximum height: 3ft 3ins – 3ft 6ins.

JC competitions – maximum height: 3ft 9ins – 4ft.

JA competitions – maximum height: 4ft 6ins – 4ft 9ins.

Horse trials

Owners and riders must be members of the BHS and the Horse Trials Group. Riders must be sixteen years or over on the date of competition. Horses must be 15hh or over and five years or over. Riders aged nineteen to twenty-one may compete in Young Rider competitions; and those aged fifteen to eighteen years may compete in Junior competitions.

Grades

Grade III	Novice horses having won less than 21 points.
Grade II	Intermediate horses having won 21-60 points.
Grade I	Advanced horses having won 61 points or more.

Points are awarded according to the Grade and whether the competition is a one-, two- or three-day event. For novice one-day competitions they are awarded 6 points for first place down to 1 point for sixth. Open Intermediate competitions are Intermediate competitions open to Advanced as well as Intermediate horses.

Rules relating to the three phrases

Novice – Grade III

Dressage
Tests to be ridden from memory.
Riders may not carry a whip but may use a grackle noseband.
Spurs permitted.
Tests: A, B C and D.

Show jumping
Maximum height: 3ft 7ins.
Maximum spread: 3ft 11ins.
Number of fences: 8-10.
Speed: 320m per minute.

Cross-country
Number of fences: 16-20.
Course length: 1600m-2800m.
Maximum height: 3ft 6ins.
Speed: 520m per minute.

Intermediate – Grade II

Dressage
Tests: K and G (roughly Elementary level).

Show jumping
Maximum height: 3ft 9ins.
Maximum spread: 4ft 11ins.
Speed: 320m per minute.

Cross-country
Number of fences: 18-24.
Course length: 2400-3620m.
Maximum height: 3ft 9ins.
Speed: 570m per minute.

Advanced – Grade I

Dressage
Spurs compulsory.
Top hat and tails optional.
Tests: P and R or FEI Three-day Event Test (Medium level).

Show jumping
Maximum height: 3ft 11ins.
Maximum spread: 5ft 11ins.
Speed: 350m per minute.

Cross-country
Number of fences: 20-30.
Course length: 3250-4000m (three-day Advanced course may be 5000-6200m).
Maximum height: 3ft 11ins.
Maximum spread: 5ft 11ins.
Speed: 600m per minute.

For notes on fittening a horse for a one-day event see chapter 11.

Showing

Ridden hunter classes

Horses registered with the Hunters Improvement Society are eligible to compete at qualifying shows leading to the Royal International and Horse of the Year Show.

Lightweight – capable of carrying up to 12½ stone.
Middleweight – capable of carrying 12½-14 stone.
Heavyweight – capable of carrying 14 stone upwards.
Four-year-old hunters – may be shown in snaffle or double bridle.
Ladies hunter – side saddle optional.
Novice hunter – not to have won a first prize of a certain value (usually £15).
Small hunter – under 15.2hh.
Open working hunter – judged 30% on jumping performance, 20% on jumping style and 50% on ride, presence and conformation.

Hack classes

Usually thoroughbred horses with extravagant paces giving responsive, light, well-balanced ride. Must be elegant and well mannered. Blemishes of any kind will be penalised.

Small hack – 14.3hh-15hh.
Large hack – 15hh-15.3hh.

Cobs

Must not exceed 15.2hh.

Lightweight – must have at least $8^1/_2$ins of bone below the knee.
Heavyweight – capable of carrying 14 stone or over.

Riding horses

A riding horse is a finer horse than a hunter but has more bone and substance than a true hack. Some horses, however, appear as all three during their careers.

Small – below 15.2hh.
Large – 15.2hh and over.

Show pony classes

To qualify for Wembley ponies must be registered with the British Show Pony Society and hold an appropriate height certificate.

12.2hh and under – ridden by a child twelve years or under.
13.2hh and under – ridden by a child fourteen years or under.
14.2hh and under – ridden by a child sixteen years or under.
14.2hh – 15hh – new class, ridden by a child sixteen years or under.
First ridden – ponies four years or over, not exceeding 12hh; rider nine years or under; ponies to be ridden in a snaffle.
Lead rein – ponies four years or over, 12hh or under; riders three to six years on 1st January.

Working hunter pony classes

Registered ponies eligible for Peterborough Championships. Judged 50% on jumping performance, 10% manner of jumping, 40% as a show class.

13hh and under – fences 2ft 9ins – 3ft.
14hh and under – fences 3ft - 3ft 3ins.
15hh and under – fences 3ft 3ins - 3ft 6ins.
Nursery stakes – rider ten years and under.
Cradle stakes – rider eight years and under.

Hunter trials

Mostly run and organised by individual riding clubs or pony clubs. They provide a useful introduction to cross-country fences for a young horse. Fences should be solid, as natural as possible and inviting. There should be plenty of variety, including water and ditches but no traps. Usually divided into two classes: Novice, with fences of 2ft 6ins to 3ft, and Open, with fences 3ft to 3ft 6ins. There is usually an optimum time for the course and penalties are deducted for going over or under the time. Courses are usually about 1-1½ miles long.

Team chasing

These are contested by teams of four horses and riders, the best three performances to count. Each team jumps round the course of cross-country fences together (there may be one or two dressing fences where the team must jump abreast). The course is very tough and big – fences can be 5ft high. The course is usually about 3 miles. The fastest team going clear with three riders wins. Prize money is good and it is an increasingly popular and competitive sport requiring big, bold, quality horses. Horses need to be extremely fit.

Long-distance riding

This increasingly popular pursuit requires great stamina from horse and rider. Riding clubs often run pleasure rides of 15 to 30 miles. To compete in the premier ride, The Golden Horseshoe Ride, held in May each year, horse and rider must have completed a 40-mile ride. The Golden Horseshoe Ride is ridden over two days, first day covering 50 miles and the second 25 miles.

Suitability of the horse

1. Stamina.
2. Courage.
3. Soundness (feet and legs).
4. At least five years old, usually not over thirteen years.
5. Up to rider's weight.
6. Sound in heart, eyes and wind.

Preparation of rider

1. General fitness exercises, such as running, cycling, skipping.
2. Practise and become proficient at judging pace and distance.
3. Get to know horse really well so as to be able to recognise symptoms of distress.
4. Learn to read an Ordnance Survey map.

Training of horse

Long-term programme taking three to six months, depending on horse's fitness at start of programme.

Weeks 1-2 1-2 hours' walking. One day per week a three-hour hack, one rest day per week.

Weeks 3-4 Periods of steady trotting on the roads, hill work at walk, then trot.

Weeks 6-10 Longer periods of trot and steady canter. Once a week a 15-20-mile hack. Start using the tack intended for competition.

Weeks 11-14 30-mile hack once a week, $3^1/_2$ to 4 hours' work per day and a minimum of 15 miles. Work can be varied with periods of lungeing and jumping. When cantering change lead every five minutes.

Feeding

Feed $2^1/_2$lbs of food per day per 100lbs bodyweight (average hunter weighs between 900lbs and 1300lbs). Add salt to feed daily. Restrict water to half a bucket after a long ride. Do not reduce hay below 10lbs. Keep to same brand of cubes to avoid change of protein level.

General management

Due to large amount of concentrates keep a look out for skin troubles, filled legs and expect cuts to take longer to heal.

Strap for 30 to 45 minutes daily. Shoe very regularly. Rider should wear hard hat, polo-neck sweater, shoes/boots suitable for walking and running in.

Week before ride
Work out a time schedule for the ride based on the required average speed. Work the horse for shorter, more active periods to freshen and liven him up. Do one 30-mile ride at or near the required speed for the forthcoming ride. Two days before ride have horse re-shod. Evening before the ride give night haynet at 4 p.m.

Day of ride
Water and feed three hours before the start. Give no hay. Groom and tack up close to the starting time. Use the first mile to loosen up horse. At check points, remove bridle, put on headcollar, loosen girth. Remove saddle after five minutes. Offer small drink. Sponge down and rub over briskly. Inspect legs for cuts, knocks. Examine girth, saddle and mouth area for sores. Allow horse to graze for five minutes. Wash the bit. Check stitching on tack, horse's feet and shoes. Rider should wash, to freshen up, but not eat or drink very much. Allow horse up to a gallon of water with salt added.

After ride
Allow small drink and a haynet or allow horse to graze. Sponge down, dry and rug up. Bandage legs. Offer small drink, bran mash and carrots. Thereafter offer small drinks every half hour and, on a two-day ride, offer small feeds of 3lbs cubes every hour. The day after the ride, walk in-hand. Reduce feed and work gradually over next couple of weeks.

Point-to-pointing

Horses must qualify to race by hunting twelve days that season and hold a certificate, signed by the Master.

Training

Horse will already be hunting fit prior to Christmas. Race fittening programme should begin around 1st January. Horse should have two hours' roadwork followed on alternate days (i.e. three times a week) by steady canter work of up to 1½ miles.

Four weeks before the race begin fast work: twice a week introduce a half-speed gallop for 2 miles, and once a week a steady canter for 2 miles. Roadwork continues as before on the other three days.

The week before the race, carry out roadwork as before with additional work as follows: Monday – 1½ miles at threequarter speed; Wednesday – 2 miles at steady canter; Friday – pipe-opener of 5 furlongs (4 furlongs – ½ mile; 6 furlongs = ¾ mile).

Tack

Snaffle bridle (loose ring or Dee).
Martingale (running, Irish or bib).
Saddle (lightweight, long, flat seat, big knee rolls).
Possibly Australian cheeker (for hard puller). This is a rubber device slipped over the bit rings on either side of the mouth, joining on the nose and running up the face to a fastening on the headpiece. It keeps the bit up in the mouth, preventing the horse from getting his tongue over the bit, and exerts restraining pressure on the nose.
Overgirth.
Possibly bandages or boots.

The day of the race

On the day of the race, give a short sharp canter early in the morning. Give usual feed but no hay. Remove water.

On arrival at the meeting, declare intention to run, collect number cloth and weigh in (12½ stone for men, 11½ stone for women). The horse is saddled up and rugged with paddock sheet and led around the parade paddock. Once mounted, he is led to the track, cantered to the first fence, which he is shown, and then cantered back to the start.

The race is usually 3 miles (twice around the track). Riders should walk the course before the race to discover where the ground rises or falls away, where any patches of bad going are and have some idea of where they want to jump the fences.

After the race, riders may not dismount until led into the enclosure and the result is given. A sweat rug should be put on horse and he should be walked to cool off. Rider weighs in. If the horse is really fit, he can race once a week or every ten days.

Pony Club

Composed of over 360 branches in the UK and more than a thousand branches overseas. Each branch organises and runs its own competitions and also inter-branch competitions. Winners of inter-branch competitions qualify to compete in finals at Stoneleigh or Weston Park at the end of the summer holidays. Competitions include dressage, show jumping, horse trials, Prix Caprilli and tetrathlon (swimming, shooting, running and cross-country). There are also the Prince Philip Games, a team competition consisting of mounted gymkhana-type races. Winners of area finals compete at Wembley in October for the Prince Philip Cup.

Dressage tests

'N' Tests (for use in horse trials).
'O' Test.
'R' Test.
Test '81 (for use in dressage).
Test '77.
Pony Club Riding Test (No. 1) (includes jumping a small fence).
Junior Dressage Test (Pre-Prelim. standard).
Test for Pony Club Novice Horse Trials.
Team Dressage Test.
Riding Clubs Prix Caprilli Test.

Horse trials

Main competitions of the year are the inter-branch ones. A branch may send one or two teams of four riders mounted on horses or ponies. Riders should be twelve to eighteen years old. Horses must be Novice level (i.e. having won less than 21 points) but they can be Intermediate provided they have not been placed first or second in a BHS trial in the past two years. Approximately six teams compete in the area qualifiers. Courses are now fairly demanding and few ponies are scopey enough to compete successfully at the final, held over the Novice BHS course at Stoneleigh. There are also senior individual (riders eighteen to twenty years) and junior individual (riders twelve to seventeen years) competitions held on the same day.

The 'N' test is currently used for the dressage phase. The show jumping involves a course of eight to twelve fences of 3ft 6ins – 3ft 9ins. The cross-country course has approximately sixteen fences, whose maximum height is 3ft 6ins. The course length is $1^1/_2$ miles; speed: 423m per minute. A water jump may be included but an alternative fence must be provided.

Hunting

Not, of course, in any way a competition but a very popular sport with many riders and frequently used to introduce young show jumpers and eventers to jumping. In good country, a day's hunting can teach a young horse to be bold and clever.

In order to be a member of a hunt and therefore hunt on a regular weekly basis, it is necessary to apply to the secretary of the hunt to become a subscriber. This will cost at least £100 for a season and may be as much as £500 in the case of a big hunt like the Quorn. A 'cap' is also payable for subscribers wishing to hunt for the odd day (between £5 to £10). Members and subscribers contribute £2-£5 to a 'wire fund'. The number of hunt servants depends on the size of the hunt, but will include the following:

- Master (often two or three joint-masters) – responsible for the administration, not for the hounds
- Huntsman – responsible for the hounds.
- Whip (usually two) – keeps hounds together
- Fieldmaster – controls the field.
- Terrier man – has two or more terriers to go down holes when fox goes to ground.

Hunting usually starts between 11a.m. and 12 noon and continues until the light goes. Hunts usually meet on Saturdays and one or two weekdays. Starts 1st November and finishes in March. Cub-hunting runs from September to 1st November.

Preparation for hunting

Horse must be really well turned out. Plait up for hunting but not for cubbing. Tack must be well cleaned. Strap the horse well and oil feet. The morning feed should be small and given early. Give no hay and remove water two hours before leaving. Travel tacked up as it is very difficult to tack up an excited horse at the meet. Velcro-fastening travelling boots are much quicker and easier to remove than conventional travelling bandages. Brushing boots on the horse's legs may give some protection against knocks, but will inevitably become waterlogged and muddy and may well chafe.

Park a little away from the meet and walk the horse to the meet to loosen him up. You will be offered a stirrup cup on arrival. Try to stand the horse a little away from the crowd and face him towards hounds so he doesn't kick them. When hounds move off, leave a gap before following. Someone (usually the treasurer) will collect your cap on the way to the first covert.

Returning from hunting

Remember to say 'Good night' when leaving for home, whatever the time of day. The horse is usually wet and muddy. Either leave the mud to dry, bandage over lightly then brush off later, or hose off the mud and dry very thoroughly – the former method is best when the weather is extremely cold to avoid the risk of chills. It is most important that the horse is left dry and clean otherwise he is likely to suffer from a chill, cracked heels and mud-fever. Once the mud is removed, make a careful check of the horse for cuts, bangs, brushing or over-reaching injuries, thorns, saddle or girth sores or a sore mouth.

Whilst cleaning up the horse, offer a small drink of water with the chill taken off it and allow him a haynet. Opinions differ as to how the horse should be fed after hunting. Some people prefer to give a bran mash which is easily digested and others give the normal feed for that particular horse. It is probably best to be guided by how exhausted the horse is. A very tired horse will usually be over-faced by a large feed and is best given a small bran mash, perhaps with some oats added, and then, several hours later, a further feed. In any case, once the horse is clean and dry he should be rugged, probably with a sweat rug underneath his normal rugs (in case of breaking out) and left to rest and unwind. He should be checked at least once to make sure he has not broken out and a further feed can be offered then.

The day after hunting the horse must be trotted up to check his soundness. He can be walked in hand or turned out in a New Zealand rug for a short period.

7.

CONFORMATION

When looking at a horse to assess his conformation always stand a short distance away from him at first and try to get an overall picture. If your eye is drawn to one particular aspect, try to decide why: is it outstandingly good or bad, or is it disproportionate to the rest of the horse (e.g. a large, plain head on an otherwise fine lightweight horse)?

Head

In a well-bred horse the head will be fine, chiselled and with good bone structure. Its size must relate to the size and type of animal. Show ponies and show hacks must have small, pretty heads but the hunter or cob type will have a larger, stronger head. In all horses the head must be well set on to the neck. If the horse has large jawbones and is thick through the gullet he will have difficulty flexing from the poll and a tendency to flex at the third vertebra instead, making him a difficult horse to keep balanced. Eyes should be large and round – small eyes are unattractive and can denote a stubborn temperament. Ears should be small and neat. Long-eared or lop-eared horses can be good performers but are frowned upon in show classes. The horse should have a flat forehead; horses that are convex between the eyes usually have temperament problems and are not particularly generous horses to train. A Roman nose makes a horse look plain and is only acceptable, if showing, in hunter classes, but horses with this feature are very often good, genuine sorts. Nostrils should be wide and soft; narrow nostrils, especially in a hunter or eventer, are not desirable because they may limit the horse's breathing.

Neck

Should be proportionate to the horse's age and stage of training. If the horse is immature, unschooled or in poor condition he will not be muscled up over his topline, and the neck, although it may be well set on at the shoulders and be of a good length, will appear weak and even 'upside down'. Whatever the age or condition of the horse the neck should not come out of the shoulders low down, as this will tend to put the horse on his forehand. It must be of a proportionate length to the body. A short neck can be compensated for by a good, sloping shoulder. It will be difficult to make a horse with a long neck, coming out of his shoulders low down, into a balanced ride.

Withers

Withers should be well defined but not high and bony. High withers can create problems when finding a saddle to fit and they will be easily rubbed by rollers and surcingles. Saddles will tend to slip forwards on horses with little or no withers. The withers may appear ill-defined in over-fat horses or in three- or four-year-olds who have not finished growing.

Shoulders

The shoulders should be long and well sloped (60° from the point of withers). Shoulders should be flat and not lumpy or loaded and at the same angle as the pastern and the hoof.

Chest

Should be viewed from the front. Too-narrow chests give the impression that the forelegs of the horse come out of the same hole, and the horse will have a tendency to brush. A horse that is too broad in the chest will look 'bosomy' and tend to roll in canter and gallop.

Ribs

The horse has eight pairs of true ribs, attached to both vertebrae and sternum bone, and ten pairs of false ribs attached to the vertebrae only. If the true ribs are short the animal will tend to be leggy and lack depth of girth. The false ribs need to be of a good length or the horse will be 'herring gutted', with a tendency to 'run up' after hard work, and be difficult to keep weight on. The distance between the last rib and the hip bone should be no more than a hand's breadth or the horse will again be difficult to keep in condition.

Back

A hollow- or sway-backed horse may be a comfortable ride but such a back is often weak and prone to trouble.

Roach-backed horses have a prominent croup which is frequently accompanied by markedly sloping quarters. The 'roach' refers to the shape of the back from loin to croup, i.e. the spinal column at this point is convex. Horses with this feature are usually strong, tough animals which often jump well. They can, however, be an uncomfortable ride and are certainly not show horses. Roach backs are often associated with a short stride.

Long backs usually give a comfortable ride and may be compensated for by strong loins and muscular quarters.

Loins

Should be broad, strong and not too long. The loins are made up of muscles and tendons which extend from the bones of the neck to the sacrum. They help to support the spine and raise the head and neck. It follows that weak loins are a serious defect in a horse.

Croup and quarters

The expression 'croup high' means that the horse's croup is higher than his withers. This will be seen in immature youngsters who are still growing. In the mature horse who has finished growing this characteristic is a disadvantage as the croup-high horse will tend to be unbalanced, taking too much weight on his forehand. If the jumping horse is croup high he needs particularly strong front feet and legs if he is to stay sound. The quarters should give an impression of squareness when viewed from behind.

Legs

The horse should stand four square (i.e. a leg at each corner). Long forearms and second thighs, in combination with short cannons make for strength and soundness. 'Leggy' horses may lack stamina. Short-legged horses may lack length of stride and speed but often give a balanced ride. Viewed from the side, there should be a straight line from the knee to the fetlock, with tendons and ligament standing out distinctly between good flat bone. The knees should be large, flat and a pair. Elbows should be well away from the ribs, so that the horse can use his shoulders freely to cover plenty of ground.

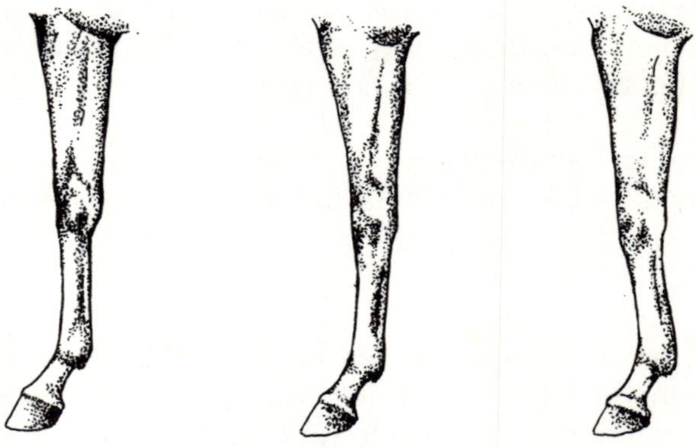

Tied in at the knee *(above left)*
The measurement immediately below the knee is less than the measurement taken lower down towards the fetlock.

Back at the knee *(above centre)*
Foreleg is concave in front below the knee. This puts strain on the tendons and is therefore a serious weakness.

Over at the knee *(above right)*
A forward curve of the knees. Sometimes seen as a result of work in older horses. Not a weakness like back at the knee

because it does not put strain on the tendons. Unacceptable in show classes.

Hind Legs

The angle at which the hind legs come to the ground influences the length of stride, the balance and the speed of the horse. If a vertical line is drawn from the point of the buttocks to the ground when the horse is standing still, and the hocks are behind the vertical line, the horse is likely to be fast and gallop well but have difficulty in showing collected paces. If the hocks are in front of the vertical line he is likely to have less speed but better balance.

Hocks

Should be large and square. If the inward bend of the hock is pronounced this is a weakness and is termed sickle hocks; this type of hock is susceptible to curbs. Very straight hocks may be compensated for by good pasterns but otherwise are often prone to bursal enlargements. The expression 'well let down' means that the hocks appear close to the fetlocks. Cow hocks (turning inwards) are a defect in showing but do not usually affect the horse's performance.

Pasterns

Should be neither too long and sloping nor too short and upright. The back pasterns will be longer than the front. Long sloping pasterns are often seen in blood horses but can be weak and make the horse susceptible to strains. Short, upright pasterns, often associated with cold-blooded cob types, do not absorb concussion well.

Fetlocks

Should give the impression of flatness, rather than roundness. Fetlocks become thickened and calloused with wear and tear, particularly with excessive work on hard ground.

Feet

Front and hind feet must be a pair. The front should be round and the hind feet oval. They should be of good sound horn and not brittle, cracked or split. Very small boxy feet are suspect, and the horse may have, or be developing, an arthritic condition in the foot. Large, open feet may be accompanied by flat soles and the horse will tend to suffer from bruised soles or corns. The frog should be large and soft. Feet showing rings or lines around the outside wall may mean that the horse is prone to laminitis but if the lines appear only at the front of the wall and do not extend round to the heels it may be that the horse has had a period at grass and off hard feed.

Conformation in relation to performance and assessment for purchase

When assessing a horse's conformation it is important to consider its good and bad points in relation to its intended job. A horse whose conformation is likely to render it unsuitable as an event horse may have conformation which will make it satisfactory as, say, a hunter or a dressage horse. The other factor to be borne in mind when assessing a horse's value is temperament. Some horses, though extremely correct in their conformation, lack such qualities as generosity, courage, level-headedness and intelligence, and they turn into that frustrating equine phenomenon – the potential superstar that never makes the grade.

So given that a good physique must always be linked with a sound brain here are some guidelines to follow when trying to decide whether a horse is conformationally suited to his intended job and he is therefore a sound buy.

The dressage horse

- His conformation must allow him to be a free and well-balanced mover.
- Strong hindquarters.
- Strong well-let-down hocks.
- Good shoulder and not tied in at elbow.
- Wither definitely higher than croup and well defined, otherwise problems with saddle coming forwards.
- Neck coming out of shoulder reasonably high up and neck

neither too long (the contact is then a long way from the rider who is tempted to draw the horse in towards him) nor too short, which gives an unattractive outline.

- Sufficient bone for bodyweight.
- Good, strong, well-shaped feet.

The show jumper

- Several famous names have unorthodox and even ugly conformation.
- Such cosmetic niceties as Roman noses and goose rumps are no drawback.
- Really good feet.
- Strong hindquarters and hind legs.
- Good front legs (not back at knee), fetlocks and strong pasterns.
- Many long-backed horses are good jumpers.

The event horse

- Needs to be a horse of quality combined with substance.
- Strong hindquarters and hind legs – can be set back a little to give speed: horse trials dressage does not demand any high degree of collection.
- Very good feet.
- Very correct front legs including length and slope of pasterns.
- Strong loins to carry $11^1/_2$ stone minimum in three-day competitions.

The show horse

- Conformation as close to the textbook as possible combined with presence. The hunter and cob can get by with a head that is a little plain if it is in proportion and well set on. Hacks and show ponies need to have really attractive, relatively small, very quality heads set on to a good length of neck.
- Sloping shoulders.
- Well ribbed, therefore easy to maintain in show condition.
- Good hindquarters.
- Well-let-down knees and hocks.
- Must move absolutely straight.

8.

LAMENESS

Diagnosis of lameness

Whilst it is unwise and impractical to attempt to be a vet to one's horses it is essential to identify on which leg the horse is lame. It is useful to be able to recognise common, easily treated minor lamenesses and to know when the trouble is more serious and the horse requires treatment by the vet.

If the horse is stabled, try to look at him first in the box and note how he is standing (do this without going into the box and so causing him to move from the position he has adopted at rest). Is he standing, resting or pointing a leg? Many horses will rest a hind leg whilst relaxing and this is usually of little significance, particularly if they rest alternate hind legs equally. Having noticed how the horse is standing in the box, have him led out so that you can have a look at his legs and feet before he is run up.

Take your time. Using both hands carefully examine the front and hind legs as a pair. You are looking for differences and contrasts in heat, shape and sensitivity between the two front or the two back legs. If the pair is not identical in these respects then you may have found the source of lameness. Bear this is in mind when you see the horse trotted up. However, some lumps and bumps are old and chronic and will not be affecting the action of the horse.

If there is no obvious wound, swelling or lump which takes your eye, ask to have him walked away from you and then trotted back. It is important that the person leading the horse neither hurries the horse from a steady jog (a famous way of masking slight lameness) nor holds tightly on to his head thus slightly masking any nodding of the head. If the horse is lame in walk, there should be no reason to ask him to trot. If he is walking lame there should be some pretty obvious signs as to the cause of such a severe lameness. The horse should be trotted slowly on a loose lead rope on a flat, hard surface (preferably tarmac or concrete).

First, try to decide whether he is lame at the front or behind or possibly both. Obviously it is best to stand in front of a horse which is lame in front, and to the rear of one that is lame behind. Assuming first that the horse is lame in front, his head will drop as the sound leg comes to the ground and be raised when his lame leg comes to the ground. Having noted which leg he is lame on, start slowly and carefully to examine the lame leg and foot and compare it with the opposite leg and foot. Lameness in the front more often than not comes from the foot, but work downwards from the shoulder in your examination. Often it is a case of slowly eliminating the possibilities. Naturally, an absolutely positive diagnosis is not possible every time. For example, you may suspect that the horse has serious foot trouble such as navicular, but this can only be certainly diagnosed by X-ray.

Whilst the most common cause of lameness in the front is trouble within the foot, the most common causes of lameness behind are the hock and the back. When the horse is lame behind, the hip on the sound side appears to drop when the horse is trotted away from you. In some, but not all, hind leg lamenesses the horse's head will nod, but unlike foreleg lameness the head will rise when the sound leg comes to the ground.

Types of lameness

Shoulder lameness

A problem in the shoulder area is sometimes blamed for lameness when there are no positive signs of injury or damage. Unless the horse is known to have slipped up and/or fallen badly, this is an unlikely reason for lameness. If the horse is suffering from shoulder lameness he should show real discomfort or pain when his foreleg on the lame side is picked up and extended as far forward as possible. If there is any degree of muscular strain the horse will pull backwards and may even rear.

Strained and sprained tendons and ligaments

If there is no heat or pain or swelling the horse has not strained a tendon, even mildly. Strains can vary in their degree of severity from the very mild strain where the horse is slightly but distinctly lame in trot to the more severe case where the horse has broken down on a leg, is almost unable to put it to the ground and is severely lame at walk. The expression broken down is often misused: if used accurately it means that the strain is so severe that there is a partial or complete rupture of a tendon or ligament. With any strain there will be heat in the area, it will be tender to the touch and there will be some degree of swelling. Swelling of the leg is not always due to strain. If the swelling does not 'pit' on pressure then the swelling is caused by infection, either from the foot and travelling up the leg, or as a result of an undetected or untreated minor wound or thorn. If the swelling is due to infection rather than strain it is likely to be more localised and affect one side of the leg.

Splints

Small bony enlargements on the cannon bone. They usually occur in young, immature horses up to the age of six years, but are occasionally seen in older horses as a result of a knock or blow. They can also appear on the hind legs but this is less common than on the forelegs. There may be very little to indicate that a splint is forming though the horse may be distinctly lame. On careful examination the horse will be found to have a tender spot when the thumb and second finger are run gently but firmly along both sides of the cannon bone. Splints rarely cause lameness once formed and hardened, unless they are very high up under the knee and so interfere with the tendons and ligaments.

Big knee

A blow or knock on the knee will usually result in considerable swelling. If the horse is not rested and treated the swelling may become permanent and calloused. The horse is often lame when the bruising is fresh but a big knee that is cold and hard to the touch rarely causes lameness.

Ringbone

Small bony lumps in the pastern area. They usually occur in older horses as a result of concussion. The heavier type of horse seems particularly prone. The condition is definitely progressive and though lameness may be intermittent, the condition usually terminates the horse's working life.

Low ringbone, which occurs on the short pastern bone, cannot be seen or felt and is only diagnosed by X-ray.

Sidebone

Ossification of the lateral cartilages. If the thumb and first finger are pushed into the coronary band it should feel slightly soft and resilient; where sidebone is present the area will feel hard and unyielding. This condition very often causes no trouble in a young horse once the sidebone has resolved and hardened. It is more likely to cause lameness in older horses.

Lameness in the foot

The horse is likely to stand favouring the foot which has the problem (i.e. he will not quite put his full weight on to that side). There may be slight or very great heat in one foot when compared with its opposite number. If the feet are not a pair, the smaller foot must be suspect. It may well have an arthritic condition such as navicular, pedal ostitis or low ringbone. If the feet are a pair and of a normal size and shape, check carefully for a picked up nail or stone. If the trouble is a result of bad shoeing, i.e. nail bind or prick, the horse will flinch if the wall of the foot is tapped lightly with a hammer. If the sole of the foot is bruised or he is suffering from a corn, he will flinch when the underside of the foot and shoe are tapped. Sudden acute lameness in the foot is usually brought on by pus accumulating within the foot as a result of nail prick or an undetected puncture wound of the sole.

Hock lameness

Bone spavin

Small bony enlargement on the lower inner aspect of the hock, best seen standing at the front of the horse and looking between the two forelegs. Once formed and hardened in a young horse they may not cause lameness, or anyway not for some considerable time. They are, however, a very common cause of lameness which may be chronic or intermittent. The horse will be most obviously lame when he is turned in a small circle with the lame leg on the outside of the circle. Forced flexion of the joint (the so-called 'spavin test') will usually increase lameness. The hock is held as flexed as possible for two minutes and then the horse is immediately trotted forwards. With occult spavin there is no bony growth to be seen as the arthritis is on the articular surfaces of the joint. In this type of spavin the lameness is continuous.

Bursal enlargements

Bog spavin (a soft spongy swelling on the front of the hock) and thoroughpin (a soft swelling on the outer and/or inner sides of the hock) are both enlargements of the bursa due to concussion and strain. Unlike bone spavins, bog spavins, unless they become unduly large and tense, do not normally cause lameness. They are, however, an indication that the horse has been subjected to a fair amount of wear and tear which in itself may cause more serious conditions in that particular horse. Thoroughpins, when small and soft, do not usually give trouble. They have, however, a tendency to become bigger and so eventually cause interference with the free movement of the hock joint, so causing lameness.

Curbs

A curb is a strain of the ligament passing over the back of the hock. The horse may be lame initially but not always so.

Lameness is more marked after rest when first starting work. The swelling, soft at first and later becoming more fibrous, is on the inner side of the hock about a hand's breadth below the point of the hock. False curb is when the horse has a large head on the metatarsal bone. This may be distinguished from true curb because it is on the outer side of the hock.

Windgalls

Bursal enlargements around the fetlock joint. Most, almost all, horses of six years and over will have them as a result of work on hard ground. Very seldom do they cause lameness and many older horses have very large obvious windgalls for many years without any lameness shown.

Sesamoiditis

Occurs both in the forelegs and the hind. It is inflammation of the sesamoid bone and also usually the sheath of the flexor tendon. The causes are usually the same as for strained tendon. There will be heat and some degree of swelling. If the fetlock joint is held fixed and the pastern flexed, the horse will show considerable pain and may rear up. The lameness will increase with exercise.

Back lameness

Not easy to diagnose. The horse will be lame behind and when light pressure with the thumb and first finger is applied along the line of the spine, he will flinch to some degree when the painful part is reached. Usually best to have the vet confirm a suspected case of back trouble because it is easily confused with problems in the pelvis, stifle or hip.

Stifle lameness

May be lame in walk as well as trot. In trot may carry the leg and whilst standing may lift the leg frequently, holding it flexed. With less severe cases the quarter on the lame side will lower at each step.

Hip lameness

The horse has difficulty bringing the leg forwards so tends to swing it around sideways, dragging the toe. If trotted in hand may tend to drag away from the lame side.

9.

Grassland Management

Horses are notorious spoilers of pasture. This is particularly true where a group of horses are turned out on a relatively small area. As a rough guide, it is desirable to have $1^1/_2$ acres per horse and slightly more in the case of brood mares. Less than $^1/_4$ acre per horse can be regarded only as an exercise space. Any attempts at improving or restoring horse-sick pasture should be based on an analysis of the soil by your local agricultural contractor.

Good pasture depends on the following factors:

1. The fertility of the soil – this can be improved by the addition of certain elements, e.g. phosphorus and calcium.
2. Altitude – the higher the land the harsher the climate.
3. Rainfall – this affects the type of grasses found and the rate of growth.
4. Drainage – poor-draining clay-based land will tend to produce a high proportion of undesirable grasses.
5. Management – a combination of controlled, selective grazing with regular resting periods and a sound plan of harrowing and fertilising.

The nutritive value of the pasture depends on the composition of its grasses. Land which has a high proportion of ryegrass, timothy and cocksfoot is desirable as these are all highly palatable and digestible to the horse.

Ideal land for horses has a limestone subsoil, rich in phosphorus and calcium.

Poisonous plants are seldom eaten by horses unless they are either very hungry and turned out on poor pasture or because their diet is deficient in some essential ingredient. Occasionally a horse will actually develop a liking for a certain poisonous plant but this is unusual as they are generally very bitter-tasting.

Poisonous plants are most commonly found in overgrazed land, wet or wooded areas.

Fertilising the land

Four elements are essential in the soil for healthy pasture.

1. Lime. Essential but it is possible to add too much and upset the balance of the chemicals. Land should be dressed in March with 5cwt to 1 ton per acre.
2. Phosphate. Required every two to three years (40-60 units per acre).
3. Potash. Lime-rich soil is often deficient in potash and an annual dressing of 30 to 60 units will be required.
4. Nitrogen. Can be added artificially, but if there is plenty of clover present this will ensure sufficient nitrogen.

Farmyard manure (FYM)

Traditionally regarded as the complete fertiliser. Should be put on in the autumn and left for the rain to wash in. Contains phosphate, potash and nitrogen. Best used on fields intended for hay rather than grazing, as it will render land unpalatable for a time and may spread disease. Unless very well rotted, horse manure should not be used as it spreads worm infection. Land should not be grazed after it has been fertilised for up to three weeks or until well washed-in by the rain.

Parasites

A clean pasture can become badly worm infested in a few weeks if it is grazed by heavily infested animals. All horses should be wormed before turning out. Droppings should be collected regularly. Graze cattle and horses alternately, since cattle will eat grass rejected by horses and so dispense with the need for mowing. More importantly bullocks can clean the pasture of worms since horse worms are killed and digested in the intestines of cattle (and sheep). The worm larvae travel on wet grass, therefore good drainage helps to minimise the spread of parasites. In time, animals develop some degree of immunity to worm infestations. Cold frosty weather helps kill off the parasites. If there is sufficient growth of grass, the horse will not graze too close to the ground, where the majority of larvae are found.

Improvement of pasture

1. Drainage (ditches and artificial drains for low lying, marshy land or clay soils).
2. Harrowing and re-seeding in late February, early March.
3. Fertilising in the autumn or spring.
4. Grazing management. The grass should be allowed to grow to 5-6 inches before grazing and should not be grazed hard in the first month. Grazing hard in May will produce plenty of clover. Alternate grazing and resting until September and then rest until November. Resting periods will depend on the weather and amount of rainfall and will vary from three weeks to six weeks. Twelve horses turned out night and day will require five 3 acre fields in order to rest and graze the land. Strip-grazing by means of electric fencing is unsatisfactory and potentially dangerous for horses.

Unless the land is in a disastrous condition it is better to 'improve' the pasture rather than plough and re-seed.

Haymaking

To be successful and commercially viable considerable farming knowledge and expensive equipment are required. If you decide to make hay it is only really worthwhile if a good acreage is available and you can rely on a local farmer to do the job properly. Unless the constituent grasses and clovers are suitable, both in bulk and nutritional value, it is best not to make your own hay. Grazing of the field must cease from early April until perhaps the end of July. Artificial fertilisers will probably be applied during late March/early April. It will cost as much to mow, turn and bale a light poor crop as a good heavy one. The grass must be cut before its feeding value starts to diminish. Once baled, it is essential that there is sufficient labour to cart and stack the hay whilst it is dry. If inadequate storage is available, the hay can be almost entirely ruined and will be of little or no feeding value. Horses require the best possible hay, and if making one's own hay means that the horse receives poor quality hay, the proposition is economically unsound as well as potentially dangerous to the horse's health. Where the area of land is small, it is usually most economical to feed the grass in its growing state (i.e. allow the horses to graze it).

Care of the land throughout the year

April to June

A good time to repair, renew and strengthen fences. Post and rail fences need to be creosoted, preferably every year, but at least alternate years.

Seek the advice of a farmer you respect and trust as to whether it is worthwhile resting the land and making hay. If you decide to make hay, plan where it will be stored so that the building is free when needed and the floor, unless it is wooden, has a covering of wooden pallets or straw to protect the bottom layer of hay against mould. The land, if you are taking hay, must be rested from the beginning of April and not grazed. The farmer will advise you on fertilising (usually nitrogen). If the hay can be taken in early June then, in a good summer, you may get a second crop. Potassium potash is usually applied after the hay is taken in.

October to February

Great care needs to be taken if the land is not to be spoilt by over-use in the winter. How much you can ride on it obviously depends on the amount of rainfall and also on how well drained the land is. Sandy soils and sloping land will stand up to more use than flat and clay-based land. In any case, when riding on the field in winter try to avoid riding along the same track. Move your circle constantly to avoid poaching. The ground will suffer very badly if the horses are turned out night and day. If turned out for short periods during the day, try to turn out any excitable horses, those likely to gallop around and churn up the field, with one quiet horse who will hopefully have a calming influence.

February to March

The land will need harrowing, fertilising (lime and phosphate applied alternate years), rolling and resting for a month. (After a dry winter you may be able to do this a little earlier.) Harrowing before fertilising is most essential as this drags out the dead grass and moss and prevents a mat forming which would discourage the young grass from coming through. Harrowing can also be used as a way of controlling the spread of worms where it is impractical to collect the droppings by hand on a daily basis, which is really ideal. By harrowing, the droppings will be spread over the ground and the worms will tend to die in the sun and air, since they thrive in damp piles of droppings.

10.

Feeding

In addition to providing some general notes on feeding this section concentrates on feeding horses in hard fast work and gives a few ideas on diets for horses with either health, growth, temperament or training problems. Basic feeding knowledge, up to and including Stage III level, is very comprehensively covered in *Horse and Stable Management* by Jeremy Houghton Brown and Vincent Powell-Smith (Collins, 1986).

A suitable diet suggested for any horse, whatever his work, can only be a guide as to the amount and type of food. Horses vary enormously in their appetites and their food requirements. Much depends on their temperament and a little on their age as to how they are best fed. A small, highly strung thoroughbred may well need more food than a placid threequarters or half-bred, standing a full hand higher and doing the same work. Certain basic principles apply to these horses, however, when they are doing fast work, whether they are eventing, point-to-pointing or hunting.

What is food?

Food is edible material of a natural origin, containing nutrients which are released into the alimentary canal. These pass through the wall of the gut into the body and, providing they are of the right kind and quantity, maintain the health and well-being of the horse.

All food contains:

(a) Carbohydrates, which provide heat and energy.
(b) Fats, which provide energy and promote renewal of fat tissue.

(c) Protein, which provides heat and energy and promotes muscular development.

Table of Constituents of Common Feed					
Foods	**% water**	**% protein**	**% fat**	**% carbohydrate**	**salts**
Grass	80.0	3.5	1.0	11.0	2.0
Hay	14.3	8.2	2.0	41.3	4.2
Oats	13.7	12.0	6.0	56.6	2.7
Barley	14.3	10.0	2.3	64.1	2.2
Maize	12.7	10.1	4.7	68.6	1.6
Bran	13.9	14.9	3.6	51.0	5.7
Beans	14.4	25.0	1.6	55.8	6.2
Linseed	12.3	20.5	37.0	19.6	3.4

Factors affecting the value of any sample of feed

1. Harvesting Example: however good the pasture, if the weather prevents the hay being gathered without getting wet and/or before the grass gets too old and fibrous, the resulting hay will be of inferior value.

2. Handling Example: hay which is transported in wet weather and not sheeted over for the journey will be spoiled to some degree.

3. Age (freshness) Example: oats are best eaten less than three weeks after rolling or crushing.

4. Storage Examples: concentrates must be stored in containers which are clean, free from damp and vermin-proof. Hay is best stored on a wooden floor which is absolutely dry. If stored on a concrete or brick floor it should be laid on top of pallets. Whilst the storage building will keep the hay dry plenty of ventilation must be provided, particularly for new hay to allow for further drying and to avoid overheating in the stack.

There are two main considerations when feeding:

1. Feeding for maintenance.
2. Feeding for work.

Considerations when feeding for maintenance

(a) Palatability. Depends on smell, taste, texture and hunger of the horse. Relatively unattractive feeds can be acceptable if introduced slowly into the diet.

(b) Bulk. A total of $1^1/_2$-2lbs is required per 100lbs of bodyweight. Too much bulk will depress the appetite (important to remember when trying to put weight on a fussy feeder or a horse in poor condition).

(c) Energy requirements. Energy is required to keep the vital organs such as heart and lungs working. It is needed to maintain body temperature. Required by the muscles for digestion, and for standing and walking. Energy is obtained as a result of burning sugar with small amounts of fat.

(d) Protein requirements. With the exceptions of straw and sugar-beet, most food contains adequate amounts of protein for the repair of tissue.

Considerations when feeding for hard work

1. The horse must have enough glycogen stored in his muscles for intensive work. He must therefore receive sufficient energy-giving foods in his diet.
2. He cannot spare energy for the muscles of the digestive system. The more fibrous the food, the more digesting it requires. He therefore must not be fed large quantities of fibrous food.
3. He must not be worked for at least one and preferably two hours after feeding.
4. Since the alimentary canal is incapable of expansion, as he works harder and requires more food, his feeds must be split into four daily feeds and he must be given more concentrates and less bulk.
5. He must be able to deliver large quantities of oxygen to the muscles through the lungs and circulatory system. He must, therefore, be given sufficient and suitable food to do this. As a guide feed $2^1/_2$lbs per 100lbs bodyweight.

Compound feeding

The horse is fed entirely on a diet of nuts or a coarse mix manufactured to contain all the necessary requirements for a balanced diet. With the exception of complete cubes the horse is fed his normal hay ration.

Different types of nuts (in order of percentage of protein)

Stud cubes: used for brood mares. Also useful for horses turned out night and day in winter and for building up a horse in poor condition.

Racehorse cubes: used for horses in fast work, e.g. eventing, point-to-pointing.

Competition cubes: high in protein and guaranteed free of forbidden substances.

Horse and pony cubes: used for horses in moderately hard work, but not doing much fast work – dressage, showing, riding school work. Very useful for ponies who tend to hot up when fed oats.

Complete cubes: used when hay is either unobtainable or expensive. Useful when hay is of poor quality and expensive. Very beneficial to horses with a hay allergy and other wind problems.

Advantages of compound feeding

1. Most horses find nuts highly palatable and do not sicken of them.
2. They have a longer storage life than most traditional feedstuffs.
3. Where a large number of horses are being kept, and bulk purchase of nuts is possible, they may work out to be the most economical way of feeding.
4. For large yards they are simple to prepare and labour-saving. Fewer and less serious mistakes are likely to arise if more than one person is responsible for making up feeds.
5. In most cases, the addition of an expensive feed additive will be unnecessary.
6. Large firms, with well-known brand names, have their reputation to defend, so the quality and mix of the ingredients are guaranteed.

Disadvantages of compound feeding

1. Inflexibility. Some horses go off them sooner or later.
2. Nuts are unsuitable for horses with throat infections and

some horses when sick refuse them. Mixes are sometimes too heating for some horses and ponies.

3. Nuts are unsuitable for mixing with medicines or powders such as bute or wormers.

Balancing rations

When working out individual horse's diets use the scientific formula of 2½lbs of feed per 100lbs of bodyweight. Divide the feed into concentrates and hay according to the type of work being done:

1. Hard work – eventing, hunting, point-to-pointing: 30% hay, 70% concentrates.
2. Medium work – dressage, show jumping, some riding school horses: 50% hay, 50% concentrates.
3. Light work – hacking, some riding school horses, most ponies: 70% hay, 30% concentrates.

Use these rules only as a guide; many horses will need some adjustment to their diet. The diet needs to be constantly monitored and changed if necessary, depending on how the horse looks and performs.

Feeding programme for a 16hh horse preparing for a novice one-day event

(8 to 12 weeks, depending on individual horse, facilities and weather)

Weeks 1 and 2: 10lbs hard feed, 16lbs hay daily

1st feed	2lbs rolled oats ½lb bran or chop 4lbs hay (after exercise)
2nd feed	2lbs rolled oats ½lb horse and pony cubes ½lb bran or chop
3rd feed	2lbs rolled oats ½lb horse and pony cubes ½lb bran or chop

4th feed	3lbs rolled oats $^1/_2$lb horse and pony cubes $^1/_2$lb bran or chop vitamin supplement carrots 12lbs hay

Next 3- to 4-week period, depending on length of training programme: 13lbs hard feed, 14lbs hay daily

1st feed	2lbs rolled oats 1lb competition or racehorse cubes 2lbs hay (after exercise)
2nd feed	2lbs rolled oats 1lb racehorse or competition cubes
3rd feed	2lbs rolled oats 1lb racehorse or competition cubes
4th feed	2lbs rolled oats 1lb racehorse or competition cubes 12lbs hay

Next 3 to 4 week period: 18lbs hard feed, 12lbs hay daily

1st feed	2lbs rolled oats 2lbs racehorse or competition cubes 2lbs hay (after exercise)
2nd feed	2lbs rolled oats 2lbs racehorse or competition cubes
3rd feed	3lbs rolled oats 2lbs racehorse or competition cubes
4th feed	3lbs rolled oats 2lbs racehorse or competition cubes 10lbs hay

Some horses may not tolerate oats or a high proportion of oats in the diet. They may do better if competition cubes are wholly or partially substituted.

It may be impossible to get many horses to eat 18lbs of hard feed when fit, and others will not require as great a quantity as given in this chart. Generally, the fitter a horse becomes the harder it is to get him to eat sufficient quantity. The 'good doers' will always thrive on less than the highly strung and anxious types. Boiled feed is best given on the night before the horse's rest day. During the first six weeks of training, the horse may be allowed an hour's grazing and his hay ration reduced by 2lbs per day.

Feeding problem horses

Some ideas on feeding different types of horses are given below. The word 'ideas' is chosen deliberately since each individual arrives at his or her own conclusions through a theoretical knowledge coupled with practical experience. Almost the only thing that everyone is guaranteed to agree on is that when feeding horses one must always be flexible when applying feeding principles.

1. Horses in very poor condition

It is important to go easy at first when trying to fatten them up. Their digestive systems will have become accustomed to meagre rations and any attempt to fatten them with large quantities of concentrates can result in diarrhoea and/or colic.

Initially give really good meadow hay *ad lib* and allow an hour or two grazing on good clean pasture. If the horse's appetite is poor a course of vitamin B_{12} injections will usually improve it. Have a worm count taken and start on a worming programme based on the results of this. Have the horse's teeth checked and rasped if necessary. Give three or four small feeds daily of chop, horse and pony cubes and sugar-beet. Carrots, apples etc. mixed in will encourage the horse to eat up.

At first the horse may be too weak to work, but as his condition improves build up the exercise very gradually taking care that he does not sweat excessively. At the same time oats, cooked flaked barley, milk pellets and boiled feeds of barley or linseed should be introduced. Really good quality seed hay should replace the meadow hay. A vitamin supplement containing biotin or methionine should be given daily – this will start to improve the quality of the horn of the feet which will probably be poor as a result of an inadequate diet.

2. Horses which are difficult to keep weight on

The problem may be due to conformation (being long-backed and/or herring-gutted) or to temperament (being worriers, excitable, highly strung or nervous). Check that the cause is neither worms nor sharp teeth. If not in fast work turn out on good pasture for several hours a day. Be sure that the horse is adequately rugged in cold weather. If the horse's appetite is poor or affected by his mood split the feeds into very small ones, giving four or even five feeds a day. Feed good quality seed hay *ad lib* or a vacuum-packed hay such as horsehage. Barley (cooked, flaked or micronised, or whole barley boiled), milk powder or pellets and sugar-beet (well soaked) are good fatteners. If the weight problem is due to the horse's temperament he will thrive when his work is not too stressful. Be patient and prepared to accept that progress may have to be made slowly; avoid over-facing, confusing and disappointing the horse. He needs quiet tactful riding and handling in the stable. Put him in a stable on a quiet part of the yard next to a horse he gets on with well.

3. Horses which tend to carry too much weight

May be due to the horse's metabolism but frequently the result of over-indulgent or over-anxious owners. It is important that the horse is not chronically overweight since this leads to heart trouble, wind problems and puts too much strain on the front legs and feet and all joints. In effect it can shorten the horse's useful working life quite considerably.

The majority of ponies have a tendency to get very fat very easily. Since they tend to thrive better living out most of the year, at least during the day, it is vital that the pasture is not rich. Indeed 'the starvation patch' may need to be resorted to during spring and summer months. If this is not available then it is better for the pony to be stabled at least for some of the day rather than become laminitic. Ponies do not need best quality hard hay; they must, however, have hay that is clean and it is easier to control their weight if they are on really soft meadow hay.

Horses which tend to carry too much weight need to be stabled on non-edible bedding – it can be surprising how much difference this makes. Greedy horses will cheerfully consume most of their straw bed every night despite liberal applications of disinfectant.

Cut out from the diet bran, sugar-beet and barley. Feed oats if this suits the horse, otherwise horse and pony cubes or a mixture of the two. Be really strict with the hay ration – if necessary reduce it to 8lbs a day. Do not feed seed hay. Grazing should be restricted to half-an-hour to an hour a day on pasture which is not too rich. Make sure that the horse is getting sufficient regular work.

4. The highly strung horse in hard work

A typical example might be the highly couraged thoroughbred or near thoroughbred who is eventing. The difficulty lies in having the horse with sufficient energy for the cross-country phase but steady enough mentally to produce his best work in the dressage arena. Because the horse will have an abundant supply of natural nervous energy he will tend to become fit relatively quickly and easily and to retain his fitness. For this reason this type of horse often does not need to be worked for as long and as hard as many fitness programmes suggest (this is particularly so in the case of Novice one-day eventing). This type of horse tends to be prone to an erratic and, as he gets fitter, poor appetite. If he goes off his feed at times it is often beneficial to reduce the work or even give him several days off – he will not lose any degree of fitness and his appetite should improve. If he is off his feed remove any feed left quite quickly and let him miss a feed or two. He should then feel hungry again, but offer him rather less than his normal feed at first and slowly build it up again.

It is not always possible with a fussy, erratic feeder to 'follow the book' as regards his diet, particularly when he senses a competition is in the offing and during the competition itself. Common sense must prevail – if he will eat only hay and carrots you cannot force him to eat racehorse cubes. The highly strung horse benefits mentally from a daily turning out period. The pasture should not be too lush and he needs only an hour or so but the added bulk will not impair his performance.

Try not to fuss over the horse, particularly at mealtimes – he will tend to sense your anxiety and become more anorexic by the day. Give him his feed and leave him completely alone for an hour. If he has not eaten up remove the feed quietly. If he will eat his hay allow him an extra 3-4lbs of horsehage, which is extremely nutritious and very useful in this situation.

11.

Fitness for Horse Trials

Preparing a horse for a Novice one-day event

Stable Management

1. The Stable Since an event horse must be very clear in his wind it is essential that his stable is sufficiently large and really well ventilated. If he is able to look out on to an interesting view of the yard and other horses, it will add to his general well-being and mental contentment and may help prevent him acquiring undesirable stable vices.

2. The Bed It is frequently necessary to bed event horses down on absorbent bedding rather than straw, which is often dusty and is readily eaten by many horses, with injurious effect to their wind. A dust-free environment will help him stay clear in his wind and obviate the possibility of bed eating and so obtaining too much bulk in his diet. Shavings (provided they are not dusty), peat or paper are all suitable. Since he must be encouraged to lie down as much as possible in order to rest his legs and feet, which will be under considerable strain, particularly if the ground is hard, his bed should be really deep and dry.

3. Hay If possible, it is best to keep the horse on the same hay throughout his training and competitive season. This avoids any digestive or skin troubles arising from a sudden change from one type of hay to another. A horse in hard work should preferably be given hard hay, but in any event the hay must be perfectly clean and free from dust and mould. Horses with wind problems should be fed their hay steamed or soaked in a tub of water for several hours. As the horse gets further into his training programme and the work becomes faster, the hay must be reduced as the protein is increased, so that the diet is not too bulky.

4. Strapping The horse should be thoroughly groomed every day (about 45 minutes if the groom is efficient). This will keep the pores free from dirt and daily wisping or banging will promote the muscular development. Great care should be taken to leave the horse dry and clean if he returns to the stable hot after work. In hot weather, the easiest solution is to hose him down, sweat scrape and either walk in hand to dry him off or turn him out in a small, quiet, not too lush paddock. The horse that breaks out after hard work may be helped by the addition of dendritic salt in the feed or by the new version of sweat rug which, instead of being made of cotton mesh, is made of very highly absorbent material which really does keep the horse warm in winter and cool in summer, in addition to absorbing the sweat and leaving the horse dry and clean.

5. Bandages An event horse will often show some wear and tear on his legs. It is important to know your horse's legs really well, their normal shape and temperature and the size and position of existing lumps and bumps. In this way you will be immediately aware of any danger signs of imminent leg trouble. In order to keep the legs as cool and clean as possible, hose them after work and use leg wash or Amoricaine. Stable bandages at night are beneficial.

6. Shoeing The event horse will require shoeing absolutely regularly. The shoeing interval will depend on how strong or brittle his feet are, how much roadwork his training programme includes and the state of the ground he is worked on, but is usually three to five weeks. He will need stud holes in his shoes. Some people prefer them only in the outside heel behind, others prefer them in the quarter front as well. The stud holes must be kept clean and plugged with cotton wool soaked in oil. The holes must be cleaned and re-plugged before each competition. This saves time at the event when the horse may be more difficult to handle.

In addition to these basic stable management duties, it is really important to get to know your horse's normal habits, for example, his attitude in his box, how much water he drinks, how quickly he eats up, how much, and when he lies down. Any change from his normal pattern of behaviour can be a sign that he is unwell or mentally unsettled. It is most important to know his normal temperature, pulse and respiration rate at the beginning of your training programme, as the recovery rates of these activities are a sound guide as to how fit the horse is becoming.

Feeding – see previous chapter

The horse's fitness

The length of any fitness programme depends upon the condition of the horse at the start of the programme. The horse brought up from grass will need two to three weeks walking on the roads before he commences his fitness programme. The semi-fit horse in light, slow work four to five times a week will need six to eight weeks before his first horse trial. The horse in hard work, say a riding school horse, doing two to three hours of fairly slow but steady work, six days a week will need two weeks' faster work before his first competition.

Opinions are divided as to the advisability of trotting on the roads when hacking out. Some people believe it is beneficial for hardening the horse's legs and others dislike much trotting on the roads because of the concussion to the horse's feet. Short periods of steady trotting, on the level or up gradual inclines, provided the horse is well shod and has no particular foot problems, are usually beneficial. As a help, when planning routes for roadwork, the following are the normal speeds with an average striding horse:

walking 4mph *trotting* 8mph *cantering* 8mph

The following is a fitness programme leading to a BHS Novice one-day event:

Week 1

Start applying leg wash to strengthen tendons and saline solution on back and girth. The term roadwork is used to cover hacks on the road, riding on tracks in trot and canter, up and down hills, through woods etc., and includes jumping a wide variety of smallish natural obstacles such as ditches, post and rails, hedges, logs and banks.

Twenty minutes flatwork, followed by ½hr walking on the road each day. One rest day per week when the horse is walked in hand for 20 mins or turned out in not too lush a field for ½hr provided the weather and state of the ground are suitable.

Week 2

½hr flatwork, followed by ½hr roadwork, 5 mins trotting.

Weeks 3-5

Monday	½hr flatwork, ¾hr walking on road, 10 mins trotting
Tuesday	½hr flatwork, ¾hr roadwork including hills
Wednesday	½hr flatwork, ¾hr roads and tracks
Thursday	½hr flatwork, ¾hr hillwork
Friday	½hr flatwork, ¾hr roadwork
Saturday	½hr flatwork, ¾hr roads and tracks
Sunday	rest day – walk in hand 20 mins or turn out 30 mins

Some horses will not require daily work on the flat. They can be lunged, spend more time out hacking or given some gymnastic jumping.

Week 6

Monday	½hr flatwork, 1hr hack
Tuesday	1¼hrs flatwork and jumping
Wednesday	½hr flatwork, 1hr hack
Thursday	1¼hrs flatwork and cross-country practice
Friday	20 mins flatwork, ¾hr hack
Saturday	½hr flatwork, 1hr hack
Sunday	rest day

Week 7

Monday	½hr flatwork
Tuesday	1¼hrs flatwork and jumping
Wednesday	½hr flatwork, 1hr hillwork

Thursday	1¼hrs flatwork and jumping
Friday	½hr flatwork, 1hr hack
Saturday	dressage or combined training competition
Sunday	Rest day

Week 8

Monday	½hr flatwork
Tuesday	½hr flatwork – work in an open space and include canter for a sustained period (start with 2-3 mins and build up over next three weeks to a sustained canter of 10 mins); canter equally on both reins. Finish with ¾ mile hand gallop.
Wednesday	½hr flatwork, ¾hr roads and tracks
Thursday	½hr flatwork, ¾ mile hand gallop, 20 mins walking
Friday	1¼hrs flatwork and jumping
Saturday	hunter trial or some other cross-country experience
Sunday	rest day

Week 9

Monday	½hr flatwork 1¾hrs hack
Tuesday	½hr flatwork, sustained canter for 5 mins, then pipe-opener over ½-¾ mile
Wednesday	1hr flatwork and jumping
Thursday	½hr flatwork, canter work as Tuesday
Friday	½hr flatwork, 1hr roadwork
Saturday	showjumping and/or dressage competition
Sunday	Rest day

Week before first horse trial

Monday	½hr flatwork, 1¼hrs roadwork
Tuesday	½hr flatwork, 10 mins sustained canter hack to finish
Wednesday	½hr flatwork and jump
Thursday	½hr flatwork, sustained canter, pipe-opener hack to finish
Friday	travel to competition, light work on flat on arrival
Saturday	first Novice one-day event
Sunday	rest day, walk in hand

Just as some horses do not benefit from a daily dose of dressage so some horses will not need jumping so regularly; a few, particularly the young and inexperienced, who are perhaps lacking confidence, may be jumped lightly three times a week.

There are two seasons of horse trials during the year. They run from the middle of March until the second week in June and from the last week in July until the middle of October. A horse can do four or five events, spaced at intervals of not less than a week to ten days. He must then be rested for preferably two months.

Interval training

Interval training originated in America and has become more widely known and respected since the successes of the Americans in international competitions. Exponents of interval training claim that it not only gets a horse fitter (especially for three-day events) but also prolongs his working life because the horse is fittened in a more scientific way, so putting less strain on him. If interval training is to be practicable it requires the trainer to have very good facilities and flexibility, as the training programme must be rigidly adhered to, regardless of bad weather and ground conditions.

One of the first people to adopt this method of training in this country was Lucinda Green. The following is an extract from her fascinating book, *Four Square* (Pelham Books, 1980):

> 'Following the initial six weeks of roadwork, schooling and the general beginnings of toning and hardening up, the programme can commence. The objective is to enable a horse to reach his peak of fitness with the minimum amount of wear and tear. Accordingly training sessions, or work-outs, take place once every three or four days, gradually increasing the amount of canter work at each session. Apparently it takes between three and four days for a horse to recover fully from a work-out. To work a horse any sooner is to work a tired limb and invite injury; to work him later will benefit the horse correspondingly less as his muscles are beginning to slacken. If a horse is becoming too fit too soon, spacing the work-outs at five-, six- or even seven-day intervals will effectively slow up his progress.

The length of each of the three canters involved in each work-out and of the two intervening periods of relaxation and walking should be calculated to produce a horse almost fully recovered during the first break, and half to threequarters recovered during the second. If he is asked to work again just before he has recovered he will thereby increasingly expand his heart and lung capacity thus building up his fitness in relation. This is a more logical approach than conventional fitness-training programmes which often involves pounding on in canter for twenty minutes or more at a time.

In preparation for Badminton 1979, Killaire's interval training programme began at the end of February. Given below are details of the last seven weeks leading up to Badminton.

March	
Tuesday 6th	5 (3) 5 (3) 5 on the flat, at 400 m/min (i.e. 1 mile per 4 mins)
Saturday 10th	6 (3) 6 (3) 6 on the flat, at 400 m/min
Tuesday 13th	6 (3) 6 (3) 6 on the flat, at 400 m/min
Saturday 17th	7 (3) 6 (3) 7 on the flat, at 400 m/min
Tuesday 20th	7 (3) 7 (3) 7 on the flat, slightly faster canter: 425-450 m/min
Saturday 24th	8 (3) 6 (3) 8 on the flat, slightly faster canter: 425-450 m/min
Tuesday 27th	7 (3) 8 on hills, including three spurts uphill
Saturday 31st	Rushall One-Day Event.
April	
Friday 6th	8 (2½) 7½ on hills, including three spurts uphill
Wednesday 11th	9 (3) 8 on hills, including four spurts uphill
Monday 16th	7 (2½) plus ¾ mile gallop, on the flat
Thursday 19th	Cantered up a hill
Friday 20th	Pipe-opener up a hill
Saturday 21st	Cross-country day, Badminton

(Figures given in brackets are the rest periods between the canters.)

NB: This programme was designed specifically for a cold-clooded, fairly lazy horse. The intervening days are taken up with mostly walking and/or schooling. The day after each work-out should always be devoted either to a long walk or to resting.'

Feeding and fitness for point-to-point horses and horses involved in long-distance rides are given in the section on competitions.

What to take to a horse trial

Dressage saddle	
Jumping saddle	Spare rugs
Bridle (different bit for jumping if required)	Sweat rug
	Feed
Boots and/or exercise bandages	Hay and additional bedding
Over-reach boots	Grooming kit
Martingale (if required)	Plaiting kit
Breastplate	Buckets
Overgirth	Haynet
Studs	Mucking out utensils
Spare reins, girth, leathers	

Veterinary chest containing scissors, thermometer, cotton wool, antibiotic powder, salt, Vaseline, leg wash, Animalintex and fly repellent.

For the rider

Money	Hat	Back protector
2 pairs jodhpurs	2 sticks	Food
Boots	Gloves	Dry spare clothes
Stock	Spurs	Map
Shirt	Cross-country sweater	Dressage test folder
Jacket	Crash hat	Horse vaccination certificate (if required)

First-aid box containing aspirins, kaolin, witch hazel and plasters.

The day before the competition

- Overnight stabling has to be booked when entering for a horse trial.
- Walk the course (twice if possible).
- Collect times for the next day.
- Exercise the horse lightly to accustom him to the new surroundings and loosen him up after the journey.
- Find your stabling (not always the easiest task, so don't leave this too late – it is much harder in the dark).

Walking the course

If you live very close to the competition you may not be stabling the horse overnight at the competition. In which case, unless you have very late times it will be necessary to make a special trip on the afternoon before the competition to walk the course.

It is usually best to walk the course with one other person, whose views you respect and trust. Having several advisers tends to become confusing. Try not to panic if this your first horse trials and the fences seem huge and uninviting. They will look smaller and less terrifying from on top of a horse and they always seem to diminish once you have seen them jumped by another horse and rider. Attention should be paid to the state of the going around the course and any deep or unlevel ground noted. If it is the first horse trial for either or both horse and rider, the route should be planned taking the simplest way on the best ground, rather than being concerned with returning a fast time.

Combination fences often contain alternatives. Make sure all routes are walked and a second choice of route decided in case of a refusal. Jumping fences across the corner requires controlled impulsion, real obedience from the horse and good steering. Jumping from light into dark is frequently a cause of refusals and these fences need to be ridden with determination. Where fences are sited in woods it is essential to plan the line you will take around the trees. Where jumping into water is required always test the depth of the water for yourself (wearing wellies of course). The horse should be presented slowly but with impulsion, encouraging him to jump carefully and not too extravagantly into the water to minimise the drag on his legs and the risk of a ducking for both horse and rider.

On the day

Dressage

Work your horse in accordance with his individual needs. Make sure you have memorised the test really thoroughly. Try to keep calm and relaxed riding in the arena, particularly if your horse is tense. If you make a mistake, forget it and concentrate on the rest of the test.

Show jumping

Check if this phase is running to time. Try to conserve the horse's energy by neither over-jumping him in the practice arena, nor having him hanging around for a long period if the programme has got behind schedule.

Cross-country

Sharpen the horse up and give him a quick blow before the start to clear his wind. There is no need for lots of jumping or galloping.

On finishing the cross-country course

Allow the horse to slow down rather than pull him up sharply or drop the reins completely. Dismount immediately. Loosen the girth and walk him back to the box. Have a look for cuts, grazes and swellings. Wash down with warm water, sweat scrape and rug up according to the weather. Bandage legs. Remove studs. Offer him a short drink. Put him in his box with a small haynet. After an hour or two he may be given water and further hay.

Typical fences found in novice one-day horse trials

Ditches Many horses have an initial fear of ditches, or at least are strongly suspicious of them. The horse needs to be presented slowly, preferably from trot, at small ditches which he can jump from a standstill if necessary. As his confidence grows he can be introduced to a small jump followed by a single non-jumping stride before a small ditch. Finally a 'coffin' can be made, i.e. a post and rails, followed a stride away by a ditch, followed a further stride away by another post and rails. This type of fence is the most common 'stopper' on any cross-country course, usually because the horse is distracted by the sight of the ditch behind the first element. They need to be approached with plenty of impulsion but steadily, with the horse really forwards from the leg to the hand.

Water Event horses must jump over and into water. They sometimes also have to jump a fence standing in the water. Some horses are bolder than others in their attitude to water and for the less brave it is a case of building the horse's confidence gradually by tackling different approaches and jumps.

Trakehner A telegraph pole over a ditch. A difficult fence, requiring an accurate controlled approach because of the false ground line.

Bullfinch About half to two thirds of the fence is solid and the top is loose brush. The horse must learn to brush through the top rather than attempt to jump cleanly over.

Hay rack Gives a false ground line.

Straw bale fence Dangerous as the bales can move and roll unless secured to the ground.

Log pile Simple, solid, encouraging fence.

Spreads The degree of difficulty depends on the gradient of the approach. Jumped uphill they require more impulsion. Jumped downhill, the stride must be kept short, with the hocks well engaged.

Bank complexes Can be a series of steps or a simple mound of earth which is jumped on to and immediately off again (Irish Bank). Both require some practice at home.

Table A good solid fence which horses respect but tends to intimidate riders.

Ski jump An ascending solid spread with a drop on the landing side.

Zig-zag fence Best jumped at the middle of a point where the poles come to the ground, giving a ground line.

Hedges Sometimes with a drop on the landing side or with a ditch on the take-off or landing side. Encourages bold jumping.

Bounce combinations Horse learns initially to bounce show jump poles which will fall if he makes a mistake, later over fixed solid rustic poles at distances varying between 9ft and at the maximum 15ft. Initially small fences approached from trot, then later larger, solid fences need to be approached in a short bouncy canter with plenty of impulsion.

Park bench Lower element outwards and a higher upward element. Jumps well.

Gates Very upright and solid so needs a short bouncing canter on the approach.

Stone walls Various heights and widths.

12.

Saddlery and Tack

Bits and bitting

Any bit, whatever its type, must fit the horse. The size of the mouth does not always correspond to the size of the horse: many big horses, well over 16hh, take a pony-size bit. The thickness of the horse's tongue and the length of the bars will also affect the fitting of the bit. Thicker mouthpieces are generally milder bits, but a horse with a small mouth and a thick tongue may find a chunky German eggbutt snaffle uncomfortable: there is simply not enough space in the mouth to accommodate it. A horse with narrow bars may accept the double-jointed snaffle better than the more common single-jointed snaffle.

All young horses should begin their training in a simple snaffle and many horses work all their lives in this bit. The Advanced dressage horse will need the more refined action of the double bridle later in his career, and the keen show jumper or eventer may need a stronger bit, but there is a temptation to think that all training problems and mouth resistances can be cured by changing the bit. A change of bit may make a dramatic improvement for a day or so, but in most cases, where the problem lies not in the horse's mouth but in his lack of acceptance of the rider's leg and/or hand, the problem will quickly return. A change of bit will be lastingly beneficial in cases where the bit is either the wrong size or shape for that particular horse's mouth.

A young horse, changing his baby teeth for permanent ones, may display some discomfort in his mouth when wearing a bit so his training is best discontinued until he is more comfortable, otherwise he may well learn bad habits of moving his tongue around or shaking or tilting his head.

Any horse who continually displays discomfort in his mouth and a lack of acceptance to the contact should have his teeth checked for sharp molars. For most horses rasping of the molars once or twice a year is sufficient but a few horses need more frequent attention.

The most sensitive areas of the mouth are the jaw and tongue. If the bars of the mouth, the tongue and the corners of the mouth are constantly being bruised, either by ill-fitting bits or by the horse pulling hard, these will, in time, become calloused and so less sensitive. The horse will take a 'dead' sort of contact. When the horse is working with an absence of tension, and the muscles over his top line are supple, he will salivate more or less, according to the individual. Once the mouth is wet, the sensitive areas of the mouth become less so, thus making the contact with the rider's hand, through the bit, acceptable to the horse. If the mouth is dry, because the horse is tense, usually throughout his body, he will feel discomfort or maybe even pain. To avoid this he may do one or several of the following:

Evasions and resistances to the bit

1. Drawing back the tongue.
2. Sticking tongue out to the side.
3. Putting the tongue over the bit (very difficult to cure once learned).
4. Pushing tongue forward between the front teeth.
5. Opening mouth.
6. Crossing jaw.
7. Overbending and dropping the contact.
8. Hollowing and coming above the bit.
9. Tilting head.
10. Grinding teeth.
11. Shaking and tossing the head.

Fitting a snaffle bit

To see if the bit fits correctly, pull one ring snugly against the corner of the mouth and straighten the mouthpiece. There should be no more than $^1/_4$in outside the mouth. The bit should lie in the mouth so that the corners of the mouth have one or two wrinkles. Horses that have learned to draw their tongues back, or get them over the bit, need the bit fitting a little higher.

Factors affecting bitting

1. Stage of training of the horse.
2. Type of work the horse is doing.
3. Capabilities of the rider.
4. Condition and age of the horse.
5. Shape and condition of the mouth.

The areas the bit can affect

1. Corners
2. Bars
3. Tongue
4. Poll
5. Curb groove
6. Nose
7. Roof of the mouth (unusual with modern bits, which do not have high ports)

Main groups of bits

1. Snaffle
2. Double
3. Pelham
4. Gag
5. Bitless

The action of different bits

1. Snaffle With a jointed snaffle used with a cavesson noseband, there is pressure on the tongue and an upwards pressure on the corners of the mouth. With a straight bar or mullen snaffle with a cavesson noseband the action is the same. When a drop noseband is used in combination with a jointed snaffle, the action of the snaffle is slightly changed because there will be some nose pressure following pressure on the bit from the reins and the bit will act more on the bars, with an inward pressure and less on the corners of the mouth with an upward pressure. Opinions are divided as to whether a drop noseband with a jointed snaffle is beneficial. Traditionally the straight bar or mullen snaffle has always been regarded as a milder bit than the jointed snaffle. However, since the jointed snaffle acts on the corners of the mouth, whilst the straight bar snaffle has a more direct action on the on the bars themselves, it is claimed by some that the straight bar snaffle is more severe.

2. Double bridle The bradoon raises the head by upward pressure on the corners of the mouth, whilst the curb lowers the head and brings the nose inwards. When the curb rein is felt (i) the upper cheeks move forwards and downwards until stopped by pressure on the poll which has the effect of lowering the head; (ii) the lower cheeks move backwards and upwards until stopped by forward pressure of the curb chain in the chin groove, and by the bit pressing on the bars of the mouth and the tongue. This action can be likened to a metal slip knot round the lower jaw and has the effect in the trained horse of producing a flexion. The size of the port distributes the pressure between the tongue and bars. Horses with large tongues need larger ports and vice-versa.

3. Pelham This has an undefined action, but is accepted well by some horses provided the rider is in good balance and has some tact and good co-ordination of his legs and hands. The snaffle rein acts on the corners of the mouth and the curb rein (when used separately) on the poll and chin groove. Because the upper cheek has to be longer to house the snaffle ring it has an over-bending effect.

4. Gag Exaggerated snaffle action combined with poll pressure.

5. Bitless Primarily acts via nose pressure but according to the type may also put pressure on the poll and chin groove.

Saddles

Most good-quality general-purpose, dressage and jumping saddles nowadays have spring trees and are made in three fittings: narrow, medium and broad. Sizes vary from children's saddles of 14ins measured from the pommel to the cantle (except with a cut-back head) to 18ins. Ideally, every horse should have his own saddle which is not used on any other horse, and preferably by the same rider. A variety of horses and riders inevitably alters the shape and fit of the saddle in time.

Fitting saddle

It is impossible to tell how a saddle fits a horse when it has a numnah underneath. This may seem a very obvious statement but it is amazing how many times people attempt to do so. To be really sure that the saddle is going to suit a particular horse it is best, if you are able, to have a short ride in it. It may well fit your horse beautifully but be very uncomfortable for you (the seat is too small or the knee roll allows insufficient room for your length of thigh).

The saddle must firstly fit your horse, but it must also suit your own particular conformation. Points to consider when deciding upon a saddle for a horse are:

1. What type of work the horse will be doing. Unless he is a dressage specialist you will need either a general purpose or jumping saddle, unless of course you are prepared to buy two saddles.
2. Always buy the very best quality saddle you can afford. Cheap saddles rarely fit well and inevitably wear quickly as usually they are made of inferior quality leather. Provided a good saddle is really carefully looked after it will last many, many years.
3. The saddle must give clearance at the withers: three fingers when the rider is in the saddle. If the tree is too broad it will lie too close or on the withers. If the tree is too narrow it will perch high above the withers, will pinch and tend to slip from side to side.
4. It must give clearance along and across the backbone. Sore

backs, especially if not detected in the very first stages, can put the horse out of work for a long period.

5. The panels of the saddle must bear evenly over the muscles of the back so that the rider's weight is distributed over as large an area as possible.
6. The saddle must fit as closely to the back as possible. If the saddle lies away from the back it will move sideways when the horse moves and rub either side of the backbone.
7. The length of the saddle must suit the length of the horse's back.
8. The bearing surface of the panel must not be lumpy or unevenly stuffed. Saddles need to be restuffed from time to time, but trying to make a saddle fit a horse by putting in more stuffing or taking some out is almost always a waste of time. The panels of the saddle must not interfere with the free movement of the shoulder.

Artificial schooling aids

1. Chambon
2. De Gogue
3. Market Harborough
4. Draw reins and running reins
5. Abbott Davies balancing rein

Artificial schooling aids exist and are not uncommonly used, so however purist our attitude to training our own horses may be, it is necessary to have a working knowledge of them in order to understand the benefits and problems that occur when using them. They are in very common use on the Continent, where the horses tend to be bigger, heavier types than the English thoroughbred or part-bred. Used in the right way, for the right reasons, for a limited period of time, by an experienced and educated rider they can be helpful, particularly when retraining spoilt and older horses. Used long term, as a means of fixing the horse's head position and in the hands of inexperienced, tactless or unco-ordinated riders, the effects can be pretty disastrous.

Chambon Useful for retraining older, spoilt horses who have become very established in their way of going, i.e. hollow and stiff along their top line. The chambon looks like an orthodox martingale with a strap coming from the centre of the girth between the horse's legs, through a strap around the neck. It then divides into two, longer pieces than the running martingale, at the end of which are two metal clips. These two straps pass through two rings either side of the poll, attached to a small leather strap which lies across the poll. The clips of the 'martingale' are then attached to the rings of a snaffle bit. By pressure on the poll and the corners of the mouth, the horse is made to lower his head gradually to a point where he will have to round and use the muscles behind the saddle.

The chambon needs to be introduced very carefully and slowly. It must be put on initially very slack so that the horse does not panic and run backwards and perhaps rear and come over backwards. It is for use on the lunge only and should not be ridden in. Over a period of days the chambon may be gradually shortened so that the horse is eventually working quietly in walk and trot with his head just above the level of his knees. To obtain any real benefit from the chambon, it needs to be used daily over a period of three to four weeks or longer. Like all gadgets the chambon has its drawbacks and dangers. If used carelessly or ignorantly it can be dangerous. It does have the effect of putting the horse very much on its forehand, and the horse will not track up. To be effective, it needs to be used regularly over several weeks (it is therefore not a short-term solution to problems in training). The rider, after removing the chambon, must be capable of using his legs to make the horse (with a now supple back) use his back and hocks.

De Gogue Similar to the chambon, but instead of being attached to the bit, runs through the bit and back to the hand. It is used when the horse is ridden. It has the same action as the chambon in that it pushes the horse's poll down, rather than, as with draw and running reins, pulling the nose in. Its main drawback is that, unless the rider is very experienced and capable, the horse may well become over-bent and learn to flex from the third vertebra of the neck.

Market Harborough The Market Harborough has the usual martingale body, ending in two strips of leather with a snap hook on both ends. The hooks are passed through the rings of the snaffle and attach back on to one of three possible positions on the rein, clipping on to a metal dee. The action is simple. When the horse raises his head above the required position (which varies according to which dee it is attached to) the martingale will become taut. If the head is lowered, the martingale will slacken and the leather strips lie in loops. The Market Harborough can be an effective aid to re-schooling a horse such as a jumper who persistently hollows and rushes into fences, if used by an experienced rider for a very short period of time, say, two days to a week at the most. It is commonly used where the period of time available for reschooling is strictly limited and a quick improvement is necessary. A horse that is ridden for a long period of time consistently in a Market Harborough usually becomes very stiff and wooden throughout his body.

Draw reins and running reins Used a great deal on the Continent on both dressage horses and show jumpers, as a means of keeping the horse's head in such a position that he is unable to hollow to evade the rider's aids. Unless the rider is sufficiently well co-ordinated in using his legs and hands, the horse will tend to get very over-bent, on his forehand and broken-necked. By over-bending he may drop the contact entirely, stiffen his back and his hocks may trail out behind him.

Boots

Different types

Brushing boots Available in a wide range of materials, linings and shapes with buckles or Velcro fastenings. Most durable are the leather ones lined with fleecy material. Black rubber boots with Velcro fastenings are most easily put on and taken off and very useful when working in muddy conditions as they are simple to clean and dry. The Velcro fastenings tend to have a limited life of six to eighteen months but are still good value for money. Some imported plastic boots can be rather rigid and cut into the horse's legs at the bottom edge; they look smart, are very hardwearing and easy to clean. Any boot fastened with Velcro only is likely to come undone in wet and muddy conditions so is unsuitable for cross-country work.

Tendon boots Protect the back of the forelegs only leaving the front of the leg largely unprotected. Made of leather or plastic with various linings. Widely used for show jumping because they afford good protection to the flexor tendons but allow the horse to feel some discomfort if he hits a pole.

Polo boots Longer than brushing boots and more heavily padded; usually made of leather lined with felt.

Fetlock boots Cover only the fetlock and not the leg. Made in a similar variety of materials with different linings to brushing boots. Often used on the hind legs of show jumpers because they protect the inside of the fetlock joints when turning sharply but leave the legs exposed to make the horse more careful behind.

Over-reach boots Rubber bell-shaped boots intended to protect the back of the pastern and heel from injury from the horse's hind shoe. Very widely used for all horses jumping but disliked by some people, particularly for cross-country as there is a risk of a horse treading on the bottom of the boot and falling. Main weakness is that sometimes the boots fold back upwards.

Reasons for using boots when working the horse

1. Protection against brushing injuries.
2. Protection of back tendons.
3. Protection against over-reach injuries.
4. Protection for the inside of the fetlock joints.
5. Protection for the lower leg when jumping, against knocks from a pole.

Possible problems caused by boots

1. Dirt and gravel working between the boot and the leg causing irritation and skin trouble.

2. The horse's skin reacting in an inflammatory way from contact with a synthetic boot lining.
3. Ill-fitting boots rubbing.
4. The horse treading on his own over-reach boot.
5. Boots fastened too tightly (particularly elasticated fastenings) and/or left on too long causing pinching and bruising of the back tendon sheath.

Bandages

Whilst most people agree that it is safe and sensible to bandage the horse when he is travelling (beware of many versions of travelling boots with Velcro fastenings – they tend to come undone and fall off the legs just at the moment when their protection is needed), opinions are divided about bandaging for work and in the stable.

Stable bandages Some people hold the view that when the horse is stable-bandaged the groom may miss signs of heat, swelling and pain and that symptoms tend to be masked.

Stable bandages are, however, useful under certain circumstances. Older horses who are competing often suffer a fair amount of wear and tear on the legs and around the joints. Stable bandages help in keeping to a minimum chronic tendency to puffiness. All horses will benefit after a day's competition, and particularly when the going is hard, from having their travelling bandages left on overnight, possibly with some suitable mix of leg wash underneath. The sick horse who must be kept really warm should be stable-bandaged. Sometimes a stable bandage is used over the top of a surgical bandage to help keep it in place and discourage the horse from removing the dressing.

Exercise bandages Many people use bandages when working horses with a history of tendon trouble. Opinions are divided as to whether such bandages do, in effect, support tendons. (On a personal note, having suffered a ligament strain necessitating a plaster cast on the leg for three months, I can vouch for the fact that with human tendons and ligaments bandaging whilst recovering from the strain does make for greater comfort. Of course, all analogies between human and equine problems are debatable.)

Some people believe that bandaging any horse, not just ones with suspect legs, is a good precaution to take against the possibility of strain when the going is very hard, particularly when jumping. The argument against this practice is that the horse becomes accustomed to the support and is more likely to suffer a strain when he is not bandaged.

Dressage horses are frequently worked in wide, soft, work-type bandages. These are possibly more comfortable than many boots, there is less risk of skin irritations and they do offer adequate protection from blows and knocks from the opposite foot.

It is important to remember that exercise and work bandages badly applied can cause serious leg problems and that bandages which come undone constitute a real danger. These types of bandage must be put on carefully and conscientiously every time by a suitably knowledgeable person.

13.

VETERINARY CARE

The veterinary cabinet

Veterinary cabinets need to be of a good size, as small cupboards, crammed with drugs and bandages and other first-aid equipment, usually deteriorate into untidy muddles where it is difficult to find anything quickly. In any case, they need to be regularly tidied and out-of-date drugs thrown away and supplies replenished. The vet's number should be on the outside of the door, so that in an emergency he can be called without delay. It is a good idea where possible to have two cupboards or chests.

1st chest (equipment)

1. Thermometer (veterinary not clinical)
2. Surgical scissors (rounded and blunt)
3. Bandages
4. Cotton wool
5. Gamgee
6. Lint
7. Surgical tape (Elastoplast, useful for securing foot poultice)
8. Suphanet (used with kaolin, but not directly over a wound)
9. Large plastic bowl
10. Bucket (for tubbing)
11. Baking tray (for poultices)
12. Poultice boot
13. Saucepan
14. Wooden spoon

2nd chest (drugs and medicines)

1. Common salt (cleaning wounds)
2. Epsom salts (laxative and a drawing agent)
3. Lead lotion (cooling for legs and bruising)
4. Witch hazel (bruising)
5. Embrocation (mild sprains)
6. Methylated surgical spirit (hardens skin)
7. Kaolin (poultice)
8. Animalintex (poultice, expensive but effective and easy to use)
9. Antibiotic powder or spray (minor wounds)
10. Cough electuary (palliative rather than remedial)
11. Vaseline (preventative for cracked heels and mud-fever)
12. Pure soap (cleansing wounds)
13. Antiseptic
14. Washing soda (bruised soles and skin)
15. Hydrogen peroxide (cleaning puncture wounds)
16. Amoricaine powder (astringent agent for legs showing wear and tear)
17. Jeyes Fluid (disinfecting stables and equipment)
18. Fulcin (feed additive to combat ringworm)
19. Tenasol (ringworm spray)
20. Mycophyt (ringworm shampoo)
21. Stockholm tar (thrush)
22. Wormers
23. Optrex (eye wash)
24. Zinc and castor oil (cracked heels, mud-fever, minor wounds)
25. Red blister (used on veterinary advice for strains, splints)
26. Terramycin eye ointment
27. Bima leg gel (can be used as leg wash or undiluted)
28. Pevidine gel (minor wounds)

Injections

(a) Intramuscular
(b) Intravenous
(c) Subcutaneous
(d) Epidural

Giving an injection

Have a capable assistant holding the horse. Clean around the area with surgical spirit on some cotton wool. The syringe and needle must be sterile. Nowadays needles and syringes are normally supplied in sealed packets and are used for one injection only and then disposed of. Tap the syringe firmly several times and ensure that the air is expelled. Check that the correct needle is used for the particular type of injection. Always inject the fluid slowly, particularly with intravenous injections. The latter type of injections are usually given by a vet, but most senior staff on a big yard find it necessary from an economic point of view to give subcutaneous and intramuscular injections.

Intramuscular injections

Given in the neck, chest or quarters. Soft muscle is easiest to penetrate so some people prefer the chest. The neck is an easy area (less danger of being kicked than the quarters), but if the horse has a sensitive reaction to the injection the swelling is more noticeable and unsightly on the neck.

Subcutaneous injections

Pinch a fold of skin and put needle into loose skin (a short needle must be used).

Intravenous injections

Inject directly into an artery or vein (usually the jugular vein). Stop the blood with the thumb about three inches from the head of the syringe. Syringe the fluid into the vein and draw back the syringe until some blood is seen.

Reasons for injections

1. Reducing infection.
2. Curing bacterial infection.
3. Administering vitamins.
4. Administering painkillers.
5. Administering muscle relaxants (treatment of colic).
6. Giving anti-inflammatory drugs.

7. Administering sedatives.
8. Anaesthetising.
9. Inoculating.

Vitamin B12

Useful for horses in very poor condition because it improves the appetite. Also used for horses during a long hard competitive season, again to encourage jaded appetite. Sometimes given before very long journeys to ensure the horse arrives having lost the minimum of condition. This important vitamin assists in digestion by breaking down proteins and fats. Normal dosage is 3ml for three days.

Prevac-T

A combined injection to protect horse against tetanus and equine 'flu. 'T' stands for tetanus toxoid which is a serum that builds up antibodies to protect the horse against tetanus, should he be wounded. Two injections of Prevac-T are given initially six to eight weeks apart and thereafter the horse requires a single injection every six to twelve months; 2ml is given intramuscularly at each injection. Foals under three months should not be given Prevac-T. Horses' reactions to the injection differ (some suffer mild coughs and are slightly below par) so work should be suspended for three to fourteen days. If stored, Prevac-T must be protected from light and freezing conditions. If the horse's records do not show whether he has previously been protected, he can have the initial two injections to start a new programme, as this will do no harm.

Tetanus antitoxin

Obtained from a hyper-inoculated horse. Given subcutaneously, 6ml at a time, before operations and after accidents. A horse suffering from tetanus is given 100ml daily until improvement is shown.

Sedatives

Sedating horses should not be undertaken lightly, since some horses will react badly when the injection is wearing off and may become unsettled to the point of becoming hysterical. Acetyl is a barbiturate and calms the horse and may be used on horses before operations or on horses difficult to treat, X-ray or clip. Promazine is a muscle relaxant given subcutaneously or intramuscularly (if given intravenously it can damage the heart). Give 4-6ml and leave in a darkened box for half-an-hour. Immobilon is a tranquilliser which takes two minutes to act. The dose must be exactly related to the horse's bodyweight. Pentathol anaesthetises the horse. Horses need plenty of space when being put out as they often rush around just before falling to the ground. If Immoblin is used the horse has to be given a dose of Revivon to bring him round again. Chloroform in a bag will anaesthetise a horse or keep a horse under which has been knocked out with Pentathol.

Penicillin and other antibiotics
Many different kinds and strengths are available, some acting in the short term, others in the long term. Used to combat bacterial and viral infection. If the horse reacts against penicillin it can be given Retracyclin to counteract the side-effects.

The veterinary surgeon

Since the vet is both busy and highly qualified and his time therefore expensive, it is important to avoid firstly unnecessary calls and secondly being unprepared and disorganised when he visits. Routine treatments such as Prevac injections and rasping of teeth can usually be planned and requested well in advance, enabling the vet to include your visit when he is in your area for other calls.

Having called out the vet make sure that the horse or horses he is coming to see are stabled ready, i.e. they are not in a field some way from the yard or out being exercised. The person who is going to be present when the vet calls must have a thorough and accurate history of the problem to assist the vet in his diagnosis. This should include a list of symptoms, when they were first noticed, what work the horse had done the previous day and whether the horse has suffered similar symptoms in the past. If appropriate the TPR (temperature, pulse and respiration) rates should have been taken and recorded. In the case of wounds, bleeding must of course be stopped, but the wound should be cleaned only with cold water. It is best left free of powders sprays and ointments. Have ready any certificates you wish the vet to sign. The person left in charge at the time of the vet's visit must be suitably experienced and able to hold the horse whilst he is examined and treated. In the case of lameness the vet will certainly want the horse led in hand and possibly trotted up and lunged. It is best to plan what you are going to tell the vet in the way of the horse's history. Try to avoid being long-winded or over-dramatic but don't understate the facts either. If the horse is unreliable to handle do tell the vet so that he is neither bitten nor kicked. If you know the horse has previously been difficult while being treated by another vet say so; a twitch or a sedative can be considered to avoid accidents. Listen carefully to the vet's instructions for treatment and write them down as soon as he has left. Follow his advice strictly and precisely. Do not be tempted to take short cuts with treatments or rest periods or increase the dosage of drugs or their frequency of use. Always spend time passing on accurately the vet's instructions to owners, employers or grooms.

Miscellaneous serious illnesses

Equine 'flu

A viral infection which appears regularly and spreads very quickly; it is highly infectious. The particular virus causing the 'flu changes so it is not possible to immunise completely. However, since the introduction of Prevac-T (see section on injections) the incidence of equine 'flu has diminished, at any way until the nature of the virus changes again, when a new vaccine will have to be produced. Young horses are particularly susceptible (as with most diseases). The first sign of the disease is usually that the horse goes off his feed and is slightly lethargic and lacking interest. This is quickly followed by a cough, slight at first, but becoming deeper, harder and more frequent. There is usually a fairly sharp rise in temperature, sometimes to as much as 105°F and a discharge from the nose which is thick and dirty coloured. The vet should be called and he may give antibiotic injections for several days. Absolute rest is essential until the horse is entirely free from symptoms and then work must be resumed very gradually and carefully. If work is resumed too soon or the horse does too much too quickly there is likely to be permanent damage to his wind.

Pneumonia

Inflammation of the lung tissue. Can be an accompanying complication of or sequel to other illnesses. Usually caused by exhaustion, or exposure to cold when the horse's resistance to germs, which are normally present in the lungs, becomes lowered.

Symptoms For the first twelve hours there will be no other symptoms but a sharp rise in temperature (between 104 and 106°F). The horse will be cold and shaking with a rapid pulse and breathing. He will stand with his neck outstretched, dilated nostrils and tucked up stomach. There will be a frequent cough and nasal discharge usually two to three days after the initial rise in temperature. The horse remains critically ill for around five to seven days. He may refuse to lie down, his breath is foetid and his droppings coated with mucus.

The horse must be kept warm with extra rugs and bandages but plenty of fresh air must be allowed into the stable. The vet will give antibiotic injections. Inhalations will help and a diet of mashes, green food and steamed hay should be fed. The horse will require a long rest before resuming work.

Tetanus

The tetanus germ enters the body either through a wound or the mucous membrane as a spore. After five to twenty days, the germ starts to spread and the central nervous system is attacked. Stiffness and muscle spasms appear in groups of muscles where the germs are present. Breathing will become rapid, the horse will have great difficulty feeding and the third eyelid or haw will close almost over the eyeball. The next symptoms are sweating, frothing mouth, tail held erect, dilated nostrils and lips drawn back, exposing the teeth. The more rapid the onset of the symptoms, the more likely the case is to be fatal. If the horse lies down, he usually does not recover. For treatment and prevention see section on injections. The horse should be given no hay and fed on fluids if the jaws are locked. Recovery will take four to six weeks and the horse will not be able to work for about six months.

Grass sickness

Despite much research, the cause is still unknown. It is most common in Scotland and is increasingly rare towards the south of England. Found fairly frequently in horses accustomed to being stabled and then turned out for a period. The symptoms are lethargy, difficulty in swallowing, some evidence of abdominal pain as in colic. Inactive bowels; food and water may be passed through the nose. Death usually occurs between twelve hours and four days, if the horse lives longer he becomes rapidly emaciated. Should he survive he is usually unable to work again.

Chronic obstructive pulmonary disease (COPD)

Unlike the preceding illnesses this disease is a chronic condition rather than an acute one. It is often referred to as 'dust allergy'. The horse, very often following some form of viral infection, develops breathing problems. The first symptom to be noticed usually is a chronic cough, sometimes in the stable at rest but always at the commencement of work and often during work. The horse becomes quickly and easily tired. There is usually a slight nasal discharge and often a raised respiratory rate at rest as well as after work.

If diagnosed in the very early stages this condition can be alleviated and the horse remains able to perform his work efficiently and without distress. If, however, the condition remains untreated and even unrecognised the horse's cough will become more frequent and his breathing more distressed. Treatment of longstanding cases is less successful and the horse may have to be restricted to light slow work or may even eventually become unworkable.

Treatment consists of drugs such as Ventapulmin to dilate the bronchial tubes which will have become constricted through mucus, or Cromovet which is given by inhalation through a special machine. The horse must be given as dust-free an environment as possible. His bedding must be absorbent; his stable should be away from others with straw bedding. He needs well-damped feeds and hay either soaked for twenty-four hours or steamed for thirty minutes before being fed, or vacuum-packed hay. Where possible he should be turned out for several hours each day; very bad cases will improve if they live out entirely.

Teeth and ageing

When riding any horse for the first time, it is useful and sensible to age him before mounting. It is not always possible to be accurate to a year either way, particularly with horses of ten years or over, but you should at least decide whether the horse is a four-year-old, who will naturally be a green ride, or, say, a seven-year-old, who should be reasonably established in his basic work on the flat and over fences. If you have not had a look at the horse's mouth before mounting, it is quite easy to be misled by either a stiff, unbalanced and perhaps a little ungenerous six- or seven-year-old and imagine you are riding a very inexperienced youngster. Similarly the precocious and naturally talented five-year-old can mislead you into demanding too great a degree of collection and over-pressurising.

Ageing a horse by his teeth has always been a notoriously difficult thing, since horse's mouths do vary in their maturity. For example, a horse corn fed from birth will have a more mature mouth than a horse living out during his early years. The only sure way to become proficient is to practise on as many horses as you can. It is particularly helpful when you have someone who can verify whether your assessment of the horse's age is correct.

Points to consider when ageing a horse

1. Gently but firmly open the horse's mouth and try to keep his head still, so that you have time to have a proper look and don't make a hasty guess. Be sure to look at both sides of the mouth as they can be quite different.

2. Look first to see that the horse has got all his permanent teeth. If he has, then he is at least four-and-a-half years.

3. Decide whether the corner teeth meet. If they do, the horse is at least five.
4. If the tables of the corner teeth meet absolutely level then the horse is six or more.
5. The so-called seven-year-old hook on the corner incisors can be a guide but can also be misleading, since it can be broken off and does re-appear at eleven years. If the horse has a hook, look also at the angle at which the upper and lower incisors meet. At six years they meet at right angles and thereafter become gradually longer and more sloping. It depends on the degree of slope and the condition of the tables whether the hook is a seven- or eleven-year-old hook.
6. Having taken into consideration the corner incisors and the length and slope of the teeth, have a look at the tables of the teeth. The tables of the teeth are oval until the horse is about eight when they become steadily more triangular.
7. At seven the deep hollow depression in the centre of the tables known as the 'mark' will be smaller on the centrals and laterals than on the corner tables.
8. At eight the marks will be the same on all the tables. The hook has disappeared.
9. At nine, the tables of the teeth have lost the black, hollow depression in the centre of the tables and the horse is said to be 'out of mark'.
10. Galvayne's groove starts to appear on the upper corner incisors at ten years and runs further down the tooth each succeeding year.

Problems with the teeth

At three and four the horse will be losing his milk teeth and growing his permanent teeth. Horses vary as to how much discomfort they suffer, but almost all will have phases when their gums are red, slightly swollen and sore. They may take a rather unsteady contact with the bit or become a little one-sided in the contact. It can be beneficial to give them a short break from training so that bad habits and mouth evasions are not formed.

The horse's teeth should be inspected once a year by a vet as the edges of the molars become sharp and may catch the horse's tongue or cheeks. This can lead to the horse feeding excessively slowly and a loss of appetite and condition. The molars require rasping by the vet.

Broken and split teeth are fairly rare but cause considerable pain.

Wolf teeth occasionally grow and interfere with the bit, causing discomfort and possibly headshaking or difficulty in turning the horse. In these cases they need to be removed by the vet.

14.

Yard administration

The Riding Establishments Act 1964, 1970

Once you hire out any horses for reward, whether for instructional purposes, hacking, trekking, competing or hunting, your establishment must comply with the laws contained in the above act.

1. You must hold a licence from the local county council, the fee for which differs from one area to another. Usually the licence runs for twelve months and then you will be re-inspected before being issued with another for the following year. Provisional licences can be issued for three months.
2. The holder of the licence must be qualified either by experience in horse management or the holding of an approved qualification, e.g. BHSAI, or by employing someone qualified to manage the establishment.
3. The licensing authority will inspect your premises for suitability and will send a vet to inspect the condition of all the horses kept.
4. The horses must be healthy, fit for the job being undertaken and suitable for the purpose for which they are being kept.
5. Stabling must be suitable, of adequate size, lighting, ventilation, drainage and cleanliness must all be of a satisfactory standard.
6. Horses at grass must have adequate pasture and shelter and must be given water and supplementary feeding when required.

7. Stabled horses must have adequate feed and water, grooming, bedding, exercise and rest periods.
8. There must be adequate precautions taken to prevent the spread of infectious and contagious diseases, and veterinary and first-aid equipment must be kept.
9. Fire precautions must be satisfactory. Instructions in case of fire, together with the owner's name, address and telephone number, must be prominently displayed.
10. There must be adequate storage for feed, bedding, implements and saddlery.
11. Any horse which, upon inspection by the authority, is found to be in need of veterinary attention, must not be returned to work until the owner has obtained a veterinary certificate of the horse's fitness to work at his own expense and lodged it with the authority.
12. Supervision must be by a responsible person of sixteen years or over when a horse is hired out for either instruction or hacking etc., unless the licence holder is satisfied that the hirer is competent to ride unsupervised.
13. The business must at no time be left in the charge of anyone under sixteen years of age.
14. The licence holder must be adequately insured (see following section).
15. A register must be kept of all horses aged three or under, and brood mares and mares having foaled less than three months previously. It is an offence to use any horse on the register for hire.

Accidents

It is inevitable that accidents will occur even in the best run establishments. Procedure in case of accidents is covered in previous examination syllabii. It is worth stressing here the likelihood of claims of negligence being made following even fairly minor falls, bites or kicks. Any case for the defence needs to be backed up by a written accident report made at the time of the accident. A book should be kept for this purpose. Sometimes this is in the form of a file with printed accident report forms.

After each and every accident, whether it involves a member of the public or a member of staff or a trainee, a report form should be filled in and signed by the person in charge at the time, by the person who suffered the accident and by a witness. Information should include the following points:

(a) The date, time and place of the accident.
(b) Exactly what happened before, during and immediately after the accident.

In the case of a fall the following points must be clarified:

(i) How long had the person ridden?
(ii) How many times had he/she ridden that particular horse previously?
(iii) Had he/she attempted to ride that particular exercise before and, if so, roughly how many times?

It is absolutely vital that you obtain the right signatures on your report at the time of the accident.

Insurance

Compulsory insurance

Employer's liability
Covers accidents to staff and working pupils while they are working for you. You are legally bound to display this insurance certificate.

Public liability
Covers the public whilst they are on your premises. Some policies carry the clause that riders are only covered when wearing hard hats and correct footwear.

Vehicle insurance
All vehicles must be insured, with at least third party coverage.

National insurance
This must be paid for all employees.

Desirable insurance

- Horseboxes used to carry horses for reward (e.g. taking liveries hunting or to competitions) must have commercial use insurance.
- If large quantities of hay and straw are stored it is wise to have these insured against fire and flood.
- Tack needs to be insured as thefts on a big scale are common. Your tack room needs to be sufficiently secure, e.g. with bars on windows and really strong door locks.
- Personal accident insurance. Sensible for key members of the establishment. Provides either a lump sum for total or partial disability following an accident or weekly payments for up to two years for temporary disability.

It is usually a sound policy to consult and take the advice of an insurance broker whenever taking out business insurance.

Straying

The Animals Act of 1971 establishes that the owner of an animal has a duty to take reasonable care to see that damage is not caused by animals straying on to the highway or on to another person's land. In the latter case the owner of the land would be entitled not only to compensation for the damage to the land but also for expenses incurred restoring the horses to their owner or detaining the horses on his property whilst awaiting collection by the owner.

Communications

Good communications are vital to the efficient running of any yard. When communications are poor, delays, confusion and disasters tend to occur alarmingly frequently. There are two main areas where good communications are essential:

1. Public relations.
2. Working relations.

Public relations

All visitors to the yard, whether clients, potential clients or simply the casually curious should be addressed in a courteous friendly manner. Because most people working on the yard are very busy throughout the day it is no reason to be short and snappy when dealing with the public and it is certainly very bad for business. If people are made to feel in the way and a nuisance they will tend to take their custom to a friendlier yard.

There are several ways of advertising the business. An advertisement can be placed in the local press on a regular basis. Posters can be distributed for display in local shops, pubs and hotels. Often the local press can be invited to attend competitions or special courses the centre may be holding and some free publicity in the form of reports and photos may appear. The best possible advertisement for the centre is a really good reputation. Whilst it is virtually impossible to please everyone all the time, if the majority of clients are satisfied much future business will be gained by word of mouth recommendation from existing clients. This process, of course, also works in reverse – a poor reputation quickly spreads and once the word gets round it is very difficult to change the situation.

Livery clients need to be firmly handled but with tact and sympathy. This is always a rather difficult situation, whether the horse is on full livery, part or do-it-yourself. It is essential to have a written livery agreement stating the terms of the livery in detail and signed by both parties.

Since livery owners tend to spend far more time on the yard than clients coming simply for weekly lessons they will appreciate a welcoming atmosphere and people who have time for a quick chat. If they do not look after their horse themselves, wholly or partially, it is important that they feel able to trust the staff to keep them informed of the horse's health and well-being.

Local farmers, the blacksmith and the vet all need to be befriended rather than antagonised. If you have a good relationship with your local farmer the benefits can be considerable. He will appreciate your keeping your fencing well maintained so that horses do not stray. Any temptation to go for a quick spree, uninvited, around one of his fields hoping to be undetected, must be resisted. In return he may well offer help over buying hay and straw off the field and storing it for you if necessary, enabling you to make considerable savings. It may also be possible to rent further acreage for grazing or riding if he feels kindly disposed towards the yard.

Creating a good working relationship with the vet is dealt with in a previous section. As regards the blacksmith he, like the vet, is an extremely busy person. When arranging his visits it is important that he is given as accurate a picture as possible, not only of how many horses require his attention but also of how many will need new shoes, how many refits, how many need trimming. He will be exasperated if you continually get this hopelessly wrong as it will make a mess of his plan of work that day. Never make the mistake of playing the expert with the blacksmith – you will probably lose his services and will certainly put his back up. If you or the vet feel a certain horse needs some corrective trimming or surgical shoeing try to suggest and request the idea rather than make demands.

Working relations

Anyone in charge of running a yard must learn to be a good communicator. Head person, staff and students need to work as a team at all times. The leader of the team, the head girl or head lad, must have the respect of his staff. This results from the knowledge that he or she can carry out each or any of the yard tasks more efficiently and quicker than they can.

All staff and students should have a written contract of employment, which states their hours, time off, holidays, pay or training and exactly what their duties are. These should be in duplicate with both sides signing the contract and retaining a copy. Students and working pupils should be given a training schedule or programme showing the build up to any exams they are intending to take.

A daily yard programme displayed in a prominent position is essential to a smooth-running yard. The daily list should give all lessons and lectures that day together with such information as vet's or blacksmith's visits, expected arrivals of hay, straw or feed, new horses arriving or horses leaving the yard, together with anticipated times. Any horse whose regular groom is absent should be allocated to another person.

The office is usually the best place to display necessary wall charts to help staff to be constantly up to date in their knowledge of the details of the running of the yard. A year planner, showing exam dates, competition dates and holidays, is very useful. Two further charts, divided into weeks and months, listing all the horses kept, stabled and at grass, are needed. One could show the shoeing situation (a different coloured pin stuck in at the appropriate date to designate when the horse was last seen by the blacksmith and whether it had new shoes, refits, removes or a trim). The second chart could show the worming situation for every horse.

Other information needing to be carefully recorded and easily accessible (either in a loose ring file or in individual notebooks):

- Livery agreements
- Tack inventory for each livery
- Inventory of school tack
- Tack repair book
- Accident report book
- Veterinary visit and treatment book

Information board for yard staff

This should display weekly lists of:

- Late night duties rota
- Horse list (allocation of horses to grooms)
- Days off
- Holidays
- General yard duties list
- Important telephone numbers list (needs to be short but should include vet, blacksmith, feed and hay merchant, doctor and local hospital).

Weekly or monthly staff meetings should be held giving everyone an opportunity to discuss problems, suggest new ideas and air grievances, all of which can hopefully be talked through to a beneficial conclusion.

Planning facilities

Any new building you wish to erect, including additional looseboxes and indoor schools, will require planning permission to be granted by the local council before work is started. Planning permission usually takes about three months to come through and may, in some cases, be refused, either directly by the council or as a result of objections from neighbours. Whilst building is in progress, inspections of the work will be made by a building inspector.

Desirable facilities

Car park
Indoor school (gallery and judge's box)
Manège
Toilets with H & C
Changing room for clients
Changing room for students and staff
Lecture room
Office
PA system
Video system
Canteen
Tack shop

Manège

These currently cost between £10,000 and £15,000 according to size and type of surface. However well drained and carefully constructed their working life is limited. Wood fibre surfaces tend to have the shortest working life, particularly when in heavy commercial use. Sand is more durable though less pleasant for the horses to work on – tends to be either deep and holding or hard and too compacted. Virtually no artificial surface resists freezing in a really cold winter although the racing fraternity are currently experimenting with Fibresand and granulated plastic surfaces. If the outdoor school is intended for commercial use floodlights will be necessary at additional cost. All manèges require really good fencing of sufficient height, say, 4ft 6ins for safety.

Indoor school

Needs to be a minimum of 70 x 140ft. If intended as a show centre 100 x 200ft is necessary. Will cost £70,000 upwards according to size and whether the steel frame and asbestos walls and roof can be bought secondhand. Additional expenses will include the surface (sand and/or shavings), lighting, doors, gallery, judge's box, sprinkler system (expensive but a real bonus in summer), kicking boards and PA system. The cost of planning permission for this and any other structure will be based on the cost of the building. Rates will be charged on any indoor school unless it can be proved that it is being used for agricultural purposes.

RECOMMENDED READING

BHS publications

Dressage Rule Book
Dressage Tests (red or maroon folder)
Horse Trials Rule Book
BSJA Rule Book
Pony Club Year Book
Riding Club Rules and Year Book
Grassland Management for Horse and Pony Owners

Other publications

CROSSLEY, A., *Training the Young Horse*, Stanley Paul, 1978.

HARTLEY EDWARDS, E., *Saddlery*, J.A. Allen, 1963.

HOUGHTON BROWN, J. and POWELL SMITH, V., *Horse and Stable Management*, Collins, 1986.

KANE, J. and WALTMAN, L., *The Event Groom's Handbook*, Threshold Books, 1983.

LEIGHTON HARDMAN, A.C., *Feeding Horses and Ponies*, Pelham Books, 1977.

MACDONALD, J, *Running a Stables as a Business*, J.A. Allen, 1980.

PAALMAN, A., *Training Showjumpers*, J.A. Allen, 1978.

ROSSDALE, D., *From Conception to Maturity*, J.A. Allen, 1975.

WILLCOX, S., *The Event Horse*, Pelham Books, 1973.

BHS INTERMEDIATE TEACHING EXAMINATION

Applicable as from 1st January 1986

Open to members of the BHS who have passed the BHS Assistant Instructor's Examination.

Candidates passing the Intermediate Teaching Examination and the Horse Knowledge & Riding Stage IV Examination within the same three-year period will be awarded the Intermediate Instructor's Certificate. It is obligatory for candidates to hold a British Red Cross or St John's Ambulance (or recognised equivalent) First Aid Certificate in order to be awarded the Intermediate Instructor's Certificate.

Certificates are not awarded for the Intermediate Teaching Examination on its own. Candidates will receive a signature in the BHS Log Book from the Chief Examiner confirming a successful result.

FEE: Apply to the BHS

Candidates may not take this examination at a centre at which he or she has been training for any period during the three months prior to the examination.

Candidates will be examined in:

(a) Taking a ride of four to six pupils, showing the ability to improve the riders by teaching correct school figures in a safe and well-controlled manner.

(b) Work on the flat – preparing pupil and horse for Novice and Elementary dressage tests.

(c) Coaching jumping over show jumps and/or cross-country fences as for Pony Club or Riding Club competitions.

(d) Giving a lunge lesson to a reasonably competent rider (approx. Stage II/III level) working to improvement, including relevant gymnastic exercises.
(e) Oral theory – e.g. training technique and lesson content, lungeing on the flat and over fences and preparing rider and horse for novice competitions.
(f) Giving a five-minute lecture on a simple aspect of basic stable management as if to students preparing for the Horse Knowledge & Riding Stage III Examination and Preliminary Teaching Test, or to brief yard workers on their duties or to ensure a well-carried-out task and joining in a short discussion afterwards.

The pass-standard is half-way between that of the Preliminary Teaching Test and the BHSI.

(Reproduced by kind permission of the British Horse Society.)

BHS HORSE KNOWLEDGE AND RIDING EXAMINATION, STAGE IV

Applicable as from 1st January 1986

Open to members of the BHS who have reached the age of 18 years and are keen to improve their knowledge of horses and riding.

Prerequisites – HK & R Stage III.

Candidates may not take this examination at a centre at which he or she has been training for any period during the three months prior to the examination.

The Horse Knowledge & Care section may be taken as a separate test. Prerequisite – HK & C Stage III.

FEES: Apply to the BHS

Requirements

The candidate must be capable of taking sole charge of a group of horses of various types in stables and at grass.

He must be an educated rider capable of training and improving horses in their work on the flat and over fences.

(i) Horse knowledge and care

All the work required for Stage III should be carried out to an even higher standard of efficiency. In addition candidates will be expected to show knowledge and practical ability in the following subjects:-

General

An increase of responsibility and organisation in the yard,

showing a deeper knowledge and understanding of all the subjects previously covered, coupled with an ability to give clear explanations of their reasons for actions and methods chosen.

Horse health
Knowledge of the main functions of all the various systems of the horse's body, also of the most common organisms which invade the horse and how to control them. Signs and seats of injury causing lameness. Ability to administer/apply treatment prescribed by the veterinary surgeon and supply relevant information to assist diagnosis.

Knowledge of developing and maintaining the horse's condition and fitness and of monitoring the same for various aspects of work. Understanding the advantages and disadvantages of total or partial rest periods.

A wider yet practical knowledge of feeding and fulfilling economically different types of horse's nutritional needs.

Management and general handling
Confirmation and development of the work started in Stage III. In addition:

Simple work programmes for yard workers and for horses.

Planning facilities, their construction and maintenance and safety rules.

Knowledge of the care of brood mares, of young stock, of sick horses and of those with special needs. Ability to work a horse on the lunge.

Communications
Show an awareness of the value of good communication and public relations and the ability to work with others in a position of authority. Show a responsible attitude and an understanding of problems which may arise in daily yard work.

How to collect and collate information; interpret instructions; understand problems; impart information; build and sustain good working relations with other people.

(ii) Riding

Candidates who are considered to be below standard may be asked to retire before the jumping phase.

Ability to ride and improve horses both on the flat and over fences effectively, with style and equestrian tact.

Assessing horses' conformation, performance, present standard and problems, and the type of work for which they are best suited.

Ability to ride and train horses for Elementary dressage tests, Novice horse trials and Newcomers' show jumping competitions.

Show correct thinking and riding when working horses in a snaffle or a double bridle to demonstrate the school work required for HKR Stage III also lateral movements, half pirouettes at walk, simple changes of leg and counter-canter.

Safety aspects when riding over varied terrain and fixed fences.

Knowledge of training the riding horse from his early days as a foal, until he is ready to compete at novice level.

(iii) General knowledge

e.g. third party insurance; personal accident cover; accident reports; straying animals, etc.

Necessary reading

Further to Stage III:
Thinking Riding, Book II
Training the Young Horse (Crossley)
Management of Horse Paddocks
Running a Stables as a Business

Recommended reading

Further books may be found on the current BHS Book List.

(Reproduced by kind permission of the British Horse Society)

SYLLABUS CHECKLIST

Lungeing
Reasons for lungeing
Safety
Equipment
Jumping on the lunge
Lungeing a rider

Breaking and backing
Duration of training
The lunge work
Introducing the tack
Pros and cons of side reins
Backing the horse
Training before turning the horse away

Flatwork
Forward movement, rhythm, straightness and impulsion
System of aids
The working-in period
Assessing a new horse
The paces
Lateral work
Rein back
Counter canter
Shortening and lengthening the stride
Glossary of terms

Jumping
Gymnastic jumping
Placing poles and jumps
Grid work
Useful training exercises
Jumping a course

Teaching
The flat lesson
The jumping lesson
The class lesson
The lunge lesson
The lecturette
Discussion topics

Competitions
Dressage
Show jumping
Horse trials
Showing
Hunter trials
Team chasing
Long-distance riding
Point-to-pointing
Pony Club competitions
Hunting

Conformation
Assessing overall conformation

Relating conformation to performance

Lameness
Diagnosis
Shoulder lameness
Sprained tendons
Splints
Big knee
Ringbone
Sidebone
Foot lamenesses
Bone spavin
Bursal enlargements
Curbs
Windgalls
Sesamoiditis
Back lameness
Stifle lameness
Hip lameness

Grassland management
Factors affecting quality of pasture
Fertilising
Parasite control
Improvement of pasture
Haymaking
Care of the land throughout the year

Feeding
Factors affecting value of feed
Feeding for maintenance
Feeding for hard work
Compound feeding
Balancing rations
Diet for an event horse
Feeding problem horses

Fitness for horse trials
Stable management
Work programme for novice one-day event
What to take to a horse trial
The day before a competition
Walking the course
The day of the competition
Typical cross-country fences

Saddlery
Bitting
Evasions of the bit
Factors affecting bitting
Main groups of bits
Action of bits
Saddles
Fitting a saddle
Artificial schooling aids
Boots
Bandages

Veterinary care
Veterinary cabinet
Injections
Reasons for injections
Calling the vet
Miscellaneous serious illnesses – equine 'flu, pneumonia, tetanus, grass sickness, COPD
Teeth and ageing
Problems with teeth

Yard Administration
Riding Establishments Act
Accidents
Insurance
Straying
Communications
Planning facilities

INDEX